T0067668

A GIRL'S GUIDE TO BIBLE Journaling

A Christian Teen's Workbook for CREATIVE LETTERING & Celebrating God's Word

KRISTIN DURAN

Text copyright © 2020 Kristin Duran. Design and concept copyright © 2020 Ulysses Press and its licensors. All rights reserved. Any unauthorized duplication in whole or in part or dissemination of this edition by any means (including but not limited to photocopying, electronic devices, digital versions, and the internet) will be prosecuted to the fullest extent of the law.

Published in the US by:
ULYSSES PRESS
PO Box 3440
Berkeley, CA 94703
www.ulyssespress.com

ISBN: 978-1-64604-070-4
Library of Congress Control Number: 2020935547

Printed in Korea by Artin Printing Company through We Think
10 9 8 7 6 5 4 3 2 1

Acquisitions editor: Claire Sielaff
Managing editor: Claire Chun
Project editor: Tyanni Niles
Editor: Anne Healey
Proofreader: Paula Dragosh
Front cover design: Ashley Prine and Kristin Duran
Interior design: what!design @ whatweb.com
Layout: Jake Flaherty

To my mom. Nearly every day of my childhood, I woke up to you sitting at the kitchen table, cup of coffee in hand, reading the Bible. It's the image of you that I will carry for the rest of my life. Thank you for teaching me to be a woman who loves the Word of God.

CONTENTS

Paper Mate
PILOT
You-are-the-God-Who-Sees
Genesis 16:13

A NOTE TO THE READER

My junior year of college, I moved from Arizona to Texas to marry my high school sweetheart. Two weeks after I got there, we broke up. I didn't know a single person in my new city and I didn't have a car, so I stayed locked inside my empty apartment, panicking nonstop about the idea that I was totally alone. Although I had been raised in a Christian home and knew I should turn to God with my pain, I was nervous to actually pray, sure that it would bring me face-to-face with the depth of my sadness and I wouldn't be able to recover.

Yet one night as I lay in bed, I suddenly ached to read my Bible. I reached into an unpacked box in my closet and pulled it out, opening up to the beginning with no expectation of what I would find. I absent-mindedly skimmed the chapters for a few minutes until my eyes fixated on a verse in Genesis:

> *Then she called the name of the Lord who spoke to her, You-Are-the-God-Who-Sees; for she said, "Have I also here seen Him who sees me?"*
>
> Genesis 16:13

Immediate, heavy tears dropped onto the page. I remembered the story. A woman named Hagar was alone in the wilderness, facing tremendous rejection. God met her there and promised His provision. In response, she called Him the God-Who-Sees. And I knew in that moment that the same God who saw Hagar could see me too. He saw that I was angry. He saw that I didn't know what to do next. I reached back into the box from my closet, pulled out a pen and some green cardstock, and wrote out "You-Are-the-God-Who-Sees." I taped the paper to my nightstand and fell asleep with a tinge of comfort that God was there, somehow present with me in my grief.

The next day, anxiety flooded my mind again. But instead of hiding from my emotions and going back to bed, I opened my Bible. As I read Psalm 91, I felt emergency relief and a spark of hope. I grabbed the same cardstock and pen and wrote out a new verse:

Your faithfulness will be my shield.

Psalm 91:4

This verse collided with my heart, downloading into me some sort of blueprint to fight hopelessness. If I could remember God's faithfulness—the way He had provided for me, loved me, and protected me in the past—I could trust Him to be faithful to me in the future. Remembering God's faithfulness became a shield to protect me from sinking into despair.

Over the course of the next few months, my room became wallpapered in Scripture. I had cardstock verses taped all over my walls, to my mirrors, inside drawers, and above my bed. Everywhere I looked were truths about God. "Every good and perfect gift is from the Father" (James 1:17) went above my coffee maker, reminding me that everything good in my life—even small things, like a hot cup of coffee—was given to me by God, warm evidence of His love. "Be clothed with compassion, kindness, humility . . ." (Colossians 3:12) was taped to my closet door, instructing me that what I wore on the inside mattered, even in the midst of depression. Because my eyes were constantly reading Scripture, I began to memorize it, and my heart became strong. Courage poured into me, building me up from the inside, teaching me about who I was because I was learning about who God was.

Five years later, I ended up marrying that same boyfriend. But as I look back on that season of my life, I get on my knees with gratitude that we went through our seemingly permanent breakup. The habit of searching the Bible, writing it out, and therefore memorizing it is a practice I've brought into my marriage, my ministry, and now my parenting. And it's changed the course of my career, too. A few years ago, I taught myself calligraphy so that I could give meaningful verses to friends and family as Christmas presents. The year that my husband and I started working in college ministry, I began selling my artwork online to help put us through ministry school. Last year, Scripture art became my full-time job. And while this art career has been a fun plot twist in my life, it's absolutely nothing compared to the beauty of knowing God better, constantly pursuing Him through reading my Bible and painting His word.

My friend, I hope with all of my heart that as you read this book and learn how to Bible journal, it won't be just a fun new art form. I hope it changes your life. I hope it meets you in your own days of pain, and in your joy, and in all of your daily circumstances. I hope you see the God who sees you. Join me, and let's love His word together.

SECTION 1

getting started

Chapter One

WHAT IS BIBLE JOURNALING?

I have to admit, when I first heard about Bible journaling, I was pretty skeptical. Sure, the practice of writing and illustrating in a journaling Bible (a Bible with extra blank space included in wide margins) made for pretty pictures to look at as I scrolled through Instagram, but I felt nervous about assuming that I could draw inside the Word of God. Was it disrespectful to paint the actual Bible? Was it wrong to write paragraphs of my own thoughts next to sacred text? Although I had always underlined important passages, this was taking the interaction to a whole new level.

And also, let's be real: what if I messed up? It's one thing to smudge a painting on a piece of sketch paper that I can throw away. It's another thing to smudge a painting in the Holy Word of the Most High God, and it's not like I can just rip out Psalm 23 and pretend nothing happened. But as I began to investigate this new, trendy art form, I learned something that changed it all for me: Bible journaling isn't a new art form at all. It's been around for thousands of years, and you and I have the beautiful opportunity to join its rich heritage.

Bible Journaling Throughout History

Before the printing press was invented by Johannes Gutenberg in the fifteenth century, the Bible, like all books, had to be copied by hand. This was an incredibly tedious process, and it made Bibles so rare and expensive that the only people who could afford one were members of the nobility. In addition, most people were illiterate during the Middle Ages (including the nobility), and the Bible was usually written in Latin, so even those who had access to a Bible often couldn't read it—a stark contrast to our ability to linger with the Bible and our journals in the morning. Illustrations therefore became a crucial element, often painted directly next to the text, serving as aids for explaining Bible stories. You can still see examples in museums of beautifully illuminated Bibles, such as the Book of Kells and the Lindisfarne Gospels, their gold-leafed pages holding paintings of scenes such as the birth of Jesus and portraits of the disciples.

After the Gutenberg Press was invented, printed Bibles became more accessible and more widely translated into common languages. At this time, writing in the Bible took on a new, important role: preserving family history. Without online databases or organized government records, families used heirloom Bibles to chart meaningful information, such as birthdays, deaths, and weddings, alongside family tree information and treasured photos. These precious Bibles were passed down through the family, becoming a way for the new recipient to grab hold of the history before them, add in their own story on blank pages, and pass it on to the generation that followed.

Today, you and I have a similar opportunity. We have the chance to join a family of believers who realized that writing down our stories and illustrating verses next to the treasured words of God can deepen our understanding of Scripture. I know that my paintbrush feels a little more purposeful when I grasp that I am tapping into a practice that has been meaningful to Christians for over a thousand years! But we are not only connecting to generations before us; we have the opportunity to contribute our time, love of the Bible, prayers, findings, and meditations to those who might pick up our Bibles after us. At some point, we might share the artwork in our journaling Bibles with trusted friends. We might someday walk in on our daughters learning from our Bible study. We might someday find our granddaughters reading our prayers. There's a sense of belonging and a depth of tradition we can celebrate as we realize that we're part of something bigger than ourselves.

What to Expect from This Book

This book is divided into two parts. In Section One: Getting Started, you'll learn practical art skills that will set you up for creative success in your journaling Bible. These include a list of tools that work well with thin pages, basic brush-lettering strokes, sample alphabets and styles, how to choose a verse layout, an introduction to simple watercolor, and some of my favorite ways to paint flowers, borders, and banners. After preparing your eyes and hands to create beautiful artwork in your journaling Bible, the section concludes with a chapter on preparing your heart, focusing specifically on the pitfall of perfectionism and making a commitment to focus instead on the perfection of Jesus.

In Section Two: Bible Journaling Strategies, we'll dive into specific ways to use our journaling Bibles for spiritual growth. While Section One concentrates on the "how" of Bible journaling, these chapters lean toward the "why," as I share stories from my own life about practices such as Scripture memorization, prayer journaling, hymn artwork, sermon notes, illustrations, and written Bible study—all of which have been powerful methods for me to engage with the Word of God. Each chapter provides examples of what these strategies look like in my own Bible and gives one or two creative projects for you to try on your own. I hope these will encourage and energize you with ideas as you pursue your own creative celebration of Scripture.

Chapter Two

TOOLS

When I finally set out to put pen to paper, I had one main goal: finding tools that worked well with the fragile, thin pages of my Bible. I knew that the Sharpie markers, alcohol ink, and saturated watercolors I'd always used before would bleed right through the page, soaking into later chapters and then warping when dry. Additionally, I felt adamant that my art and words should never cover up or compete with the text. Simply put, I was determined to make sure that the words of the Bible always remained the obvious priority of the page. In order to do this, I needed the right tools.

The following are my favorite tools to use, but you should view them as a launching pad and not a limit! The perfect place to try out any pen, paint, marker, or accessory is in the first and last pages of your Bible. These pages are either blank or have information like copyright and a preface. The final pages of my Bible are completely filled with my experiments. I used the same basic blue and black colors to test out variations in acrylics, watercolors, and colored pencils, and then I also wrote out the names of pens as a quick reference guide. Next, I tested the interaction between different paints and pens, gesso layering, stamps, washi tape, and more. The pages turned out to be busier than I normally like, but it was totally worth it to feel confident about how each product interacted with the paper and other materials. I recommend using every inch of those pages as you get started on your own journey.

Any arts and craft supply store will give you a one-stop shop for buying all of these tools. I love going to a store in person to wander the aisles, compare colors, and know exactly what I'm getting; however, if shopping from your couch in pajamas is your jam, you can just as easily buy all of these tools online.

Pens and Pencils

Micron Pens

Micron pens (the generic versions are called technical drawing pens) are by far my favorite Bible-journaling tool. They are intended for precise, consistent lines, and their signature Pigma ink is specifically designed to not bleed on even the thinnest of pages, making them ideal for this craft. Additionally, the ink doesn't run or feather if it comes in contact with liquid, which is perfect if you'd like to combine writing with watercolor. Micron pens come in seven tip sizes (003 to 08), so you can choose your level of line thickness. My go-to size is 03, but I use a variety of sizes depending on how delicate or bold I want my writing and illustration to look.

I generally use Micron pens for writing small notes, such as Bible-study notes, sermon notes, prayers, and meditations (more on these in Section Two). I also use them for fine-lined illustrations, such as the anatomical heart on page 102.

Black Brush Pen

A black brush pen has been my constant companion ever since I started lettering, and I was pleasantly surprised that it didn't totally soak through the pages of my journaling Bible. Brush pens are a fun combination of a paintbrush and marker, in which the tip of the pen is flexible like a paint brush (the one I use has synthetic bristles, but some are made of natural hairs or soft felt), and the ink is stored inside the barrel of the pen like a marker. This makes it simple and portable, although I always store mine in a plastic bag when I take it somewhere—I've ruined more than one purse when ink from my brush pen leaked out of its barrel.

My favorite brand is the Pentel Pigment Ink Brush Pen in size medium. I prefer this brand because the firm, synthetic bristles give me easier control of my lettering, and I can increase the ink flow by gently squeezing the barrel of the pen (not all brush pens have this feature).

I recommend adding a thin layer of clear gesso on your page before using this brush (for more on clear gesso, see page 12), but it's not totally necessary.

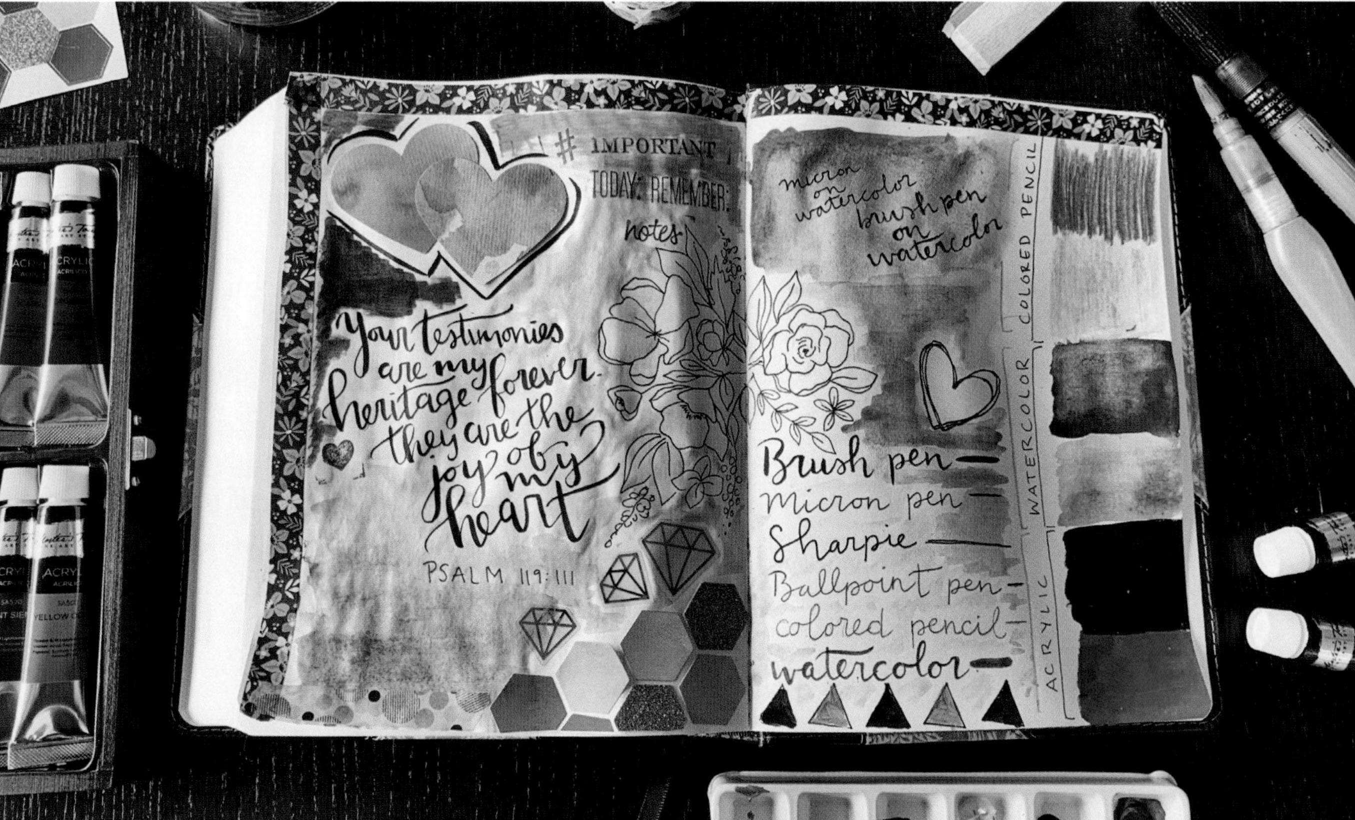

I generally use brush pens for larger writing, such as painting a verse I want to memorize or making a header for a project page.

Ballpoint Pens

I will always be grateful for basic ballpoint pens. I normally use these to underline meaningful verses as I read through the text, and it's nice that they come in a variety of colors (my go-tos are red, black, and blue). I recommend using medium- or fine-point pens. Beware that sometimes ink can build up on the tip and smear when you first put pen to paper. In order to avoid this, I'll wipe the tip of the pen with my finger or a paper towel to remove excess ink before I place it on my page.

Colored Pencils

These are a simple, mess-free way to add illustrations to your Bible. They usually provide a softer aesthetic, glide smoothly onto the page, and are easily layered underneath a Micron pen. I'm happy with basic Crayola colored pencils that can be bought anywhere, but sometimes I opt for fancier brands like Prismacolor because they're a bit richer and smoother.

Highlighters

Highlighters are a classic Bible-study tool, their bright colors immediately drawing attention to any verse they slide over. Highlighters come in a variety of colors, but yellow, pink, and orange are usually my favorite to use, as colors like blue, green, and purple are sometimes too dark and make verses hard to read. I recommend experimenting on the preface pages of your Bible to see how different colors interact with the text.

Gel Pens

Gel pens are a perfect way to add a pop of color to lettering. Many sets come with fun metallic and glitter options, but the color I use more than any other is white. It is one of the easiest ways to add highlights and dimension to colored pencil and watercolor illustrations (like the jewel illustration project on page 105). However, there are two things to watch for with gel pens: first, not all gel pens layer well. Some of them, like the mini versions, have such a fine tip that there's not enough ink flow to layer on top of colored pencils or watercolor. I use U Brands gel pens, but any set with a medium-sized tip should work great. Second, the ink in a gel pen comes out very wet, and it will smear if you touch it before it's dry (the ink is usually dry within ten seconds).

Paints

Watercolors

I generally use a combination of tubes (thick liquid paint you squeeze out onto an artist's palette) and cakes (which are dry and come in a pan with other colors). Although I'm not a stickler for any specific brand, I've recently discovered Savannah Sohne's Smart Watercolor kit, which has 42 colors, a water brush, a sponge, and a mixing palette, all in a portable pan. I love having a set of watercolors that can easily be stored in my backpack or purse, letting me practice my art whenever inspiration strikes.

Acrylics

Prior to Bible journaling, I had never touched acrylic paints. But I've grown to love the striking, solid colors that glide smoothly over the page. Acrylics don't require water (apart from cleaning the brush in between colors), which makes them a bit easier to work with. They're wonderful for painting flat, opaque areas of color as well as layering solid colors on top of each other, and they can also add nice texture to your page.

Brushes

Although there are a wide array of brush textures, shapes, and sizes, I generally stick to a small number of brushes and use them no matter what kind of picture I'm painting. The main reason is that my familiarity with a brush seems to matter more than the specific qualities of the brush. If I'm used to the way a brush feels and moves in my hand, I have better control over my picture, even if the brush is from a cheaper or less respected brand. I recommend that you choose a few brushes to experiment with, and then practice with them over and over until they feel like an old friend.

This book primarily covers watercolor painting, so my recommendations are focused on watercolor brushes (and I even use my watercolor brushes to paint the various acrylic pictures found in later chapters!). However, it's important to mention that acrylic brushes have different properties than watercolor brushes, such as firmer bristles, which absorb less water.

Water Brush

My favorite brush to use for watercolors is Pentel's Aquash Water Brush. Similar to the brush pen, it holds liquid (in this case, water) inside its barrel. You can buy them individually or in a set of three (with small, medium, and large tips), which is handy for varying the size of your illustrations or lettering.

Round Brush

This is the most common shape of paintbrush and is probably the one you used the most with your watercolor paints. It has a pointed tip for detail but then thickens toward the base, which is helpful for broader lines and curves. Round brushes are my go-to shape because I like the versatility of using one brush for multiple strokes rather than needing to change out brushes mid-painting. They come in many sizes, but for Bible journaling, I stick to medium to small brushes because I'm painting a small space.

Flat Brush

This brush looks just like it sounds. The bristles are arranged in a thin, wide square and are great for painting large surfaces that don't require any detail (like single-color acrylic backgrounds).

Foam Brush

The only time I use a foam brush in Bible journaling is with gesso (see below). These are usually made up of a wooden handle with a piece of square foam attached at the top and are great for spreading thick liquid smoothly across a surface. Foam brushes are often inexpensive and disposable, so there's no need to clean or store them in a specific way.

Clear Gesso

When I finally decided to try Bible journaling, I set out to find an invisible product that would coat the delicate page of my Bible, providing a buffer between the paper and my paint, pen, and ink so that my art/writing wouldn't completely bleed through the page. I was thrilled to discover that such a product actually exists! Gesso is traditionally used to prime canvases for acrylic or oil paint so that it doesn't soak into the fibers of the canvas. In addition to sealing the canvas, gesso provides a toothy texture for the paint to grab onto. Similarly, priming your Bible page with gesso will prevent your paint from absorbing into the paper.

You can apply gesso with a black foam brush. I've only ever experimented with one layer of gesso, but if you're extra concerned that your painting will bleed through a page, you can add additional layers after the first has dried. Be sure that your layers are thin (not goopy!) and be careful to let them completely dry (around ten to twenty minutes) before closing your Bible, as it can also act as a glue between pages. After it's dried, the page might try to curl up, but the weight of the rest of your Bible will help it flatten out once the Bible is closed.

Extras

Mat for Bleed-through Products

Whenever I'm using a liquid medium in my Bible (like watercolors or my brush pen), I make sure to place a mat underneath the page in case the liquid bleeds through. My mat is simply a piece of heavy cardstock, but anything thin, smooth, and sturdy will work.

Washi Tape

Washi tape is colorful tape that tears easily, making it popular for all sorts of crafts, and I've found it extremely helpful for taping things inside my Bible. This gentle tape doesn't leave any sticky residue behind, and it won't tear the page if you decide to remove it (although I still recommend using a gentle hand when lifting it off). The times I've most frequently used washi tape are when I've accidentally bled through one side of the page but still want to write something on the other side. I simply write or illustrate my thoughts on a piece of thin cardstock and then tape the cardstock in the normal margin space. Additionally, many people use washi tape as a pretty border or line to separate thoughts in their Bibles.

Sticky Notes

Because we are lifelong learners of the Bible, the same verse can speak to us over and over in different seasons. Sometimes I've used up the entire margin of a page with thoughts, notes, and prayers, only to find out that I have something new to write or paint and there's no more space. In this situation, I love sticky notes. I simply write out my thoughts on a sticky note and place it in the margins. Because sticky notes work like a flap, I can easily lift them up and see my previous writing.

Cutouts, Stickers, and Stamps

Attention, scrapbookers! Bible journaling is a great lane in which your paper-craft dreams can run. There are endless supplies of cutouts, stickers, stamps, and other accessory tools at any craft store. My general rule is to only purchase products that I can see myself using multiple times in my Bible. I don't want to purchase a stamp of a pretty mountain and then feel like I can only use it once! My stamp collection includes alphabet letters (for an example, see page 114), dates, banners, and other multiple-use words. Caution: stamps are notorious for bleeding through Bible paper. I definitely recommend layering gesso underneath.

Ruler

I use a ruler almost every time I work in my journaling Bible. Straight lines do wonders for making a page look put together and clean. If I'm drawing out a verse to memorize, I first use my ruler to pencil out baselines so that I can write my words neatly on the page. If I'm diving deep into Bible study, I use my ruler to draw simple squares to organize information. Rulers also help for general Bible-journaling projects, such as the Scripture Memory projects starting on page 65 and the Prayer Points project starting on page 80.

The Bible

While this one seems super obvious, the Bible is the greatest Bible-journaling tool we have. It holds a profoundly important place in history past and eternity future, and learning about it can fuel confidence in our faith that truly changes the way we believe, think, and act.

What Makes the Bible Different from Every Other Book?

THE BIBLE'S COMPOSITION IS ENTIRELY UNIQUE. It was written by more than forty authors in three different languages on three different continents over a period of around 1,500 years. The writers were from different cultures, generations, and socioeconomic classes—kings, fishermen, shepherds, a doctor, a musician, a tentmaker, and more. Can you imagine if a different book had this kind of wild variation? It wouldn't make any sense. Yet despite this seemingly disjointed authorship, the Bible maintains continuity, integrity, and a unified declaration of the gospel. The Old Testament prophesies Christ, and the New Testament proclaims Him.

THE BIBLE IS MIRACULOUSLY DURABLE. It has been burned, prohibited, attacked, and mocked, and entire governments have fought to destroy it. Yet it remains the best-selling book of all time, translated into 698 languages, with billions of copies sold.

THE BIBLE IS HISTORICALLY ACCURATE. You can personally see biblical artifacts, walk the exact ground where Jesus walked, study the actual places, peoples, and events in history books, and learn about the 24,000 manuscripts that confirm the New Testament. And let's not forget the 300 fulfilled prophecies about Christ! Furthermore, the Bible is seen as a holy book by every other major world religion, and it declares itself to be inspired text.

THE BIBLE IS STILL APPLICABLE. Despite being an ancient book, it continues to have a practical impact on people's lives around the world. As we let the words of the Bible take root inside us, it changes our character from the inside out, teaching us about forgiveness, compassion, servant-heartedness, relationships, money, time, and more. This is only one of the reasons that millions of people read the Bible year after year, making it the subject of more songs, podcasts, sermons, books, and lectures than any other topic.

Sister, start your Bible-journaling with confidence, awe, and celebration that what you're reading is the true, supernatural Word of God. Let it grip your life, change your heart, and stir your mind.

Types of Journaling Bibles

You can find a journaling Bible in nearly every translation, and most have variations in print size and columns of Scripture. The feature that sets journaling Bibles apart from other Bibles is the extra space given for writing and illustration, and so the amount of space varies between different Bibles, normally letting the buyer choose between one or two inches of journaling space in the margins. However, the Crossway ESV Scripture Journals have each book of the Bible individually bound and an entire blank page opposite every page of Scripture. My personal journaling Bible is Crossway's ESV Single Column Journaling Bible in the Antique Floral Design.

Your Workspace

While many art forms require a designated workspace, you don't need any specific setup to get started with Bible journaling. In fact, you'll most likely use your Bible journal in a few different places, including church, coffee shops, and your home. Some projects require a tiny bit of extra preparation (such as having a cup of water for watercolor paint), but these are still easy to take from place to place, and all of the Bible-journaling tools mentioned above are small enough to fit into a backpack. The most important thing is that no matter where you settle in for some Bible-journaling time, your space feels comfortable and focused. For me, this means a clean, organized area where I'm free from distractions. In order to get my mind into an artistic zone, I also love to pour myself some hot tea, play some worship music, and turn on some soft lighting instead of relying on bright overhead lights.

Chapter Three

INTRODUCTION TO HAND LETTERING

Brush Pen Lettering

A few years into writing Bible verses on cardstock, I was a brand-new wife and wanting a fun (and free) hobby I could do while my husband worked late. I had seen people post pretty quotes in pretty lettering online, and I thought, "I can do that." After watching a few YouTube videos, I got out a pencil and started copying fonts. I realized from the beginning that it was going to take a significant amount of time for lettering to come naturally, and so I decided that I would use an entire sketchbook as scratch paper, messing up as often and boldly as needed, no matter how ugly the results.

At the time, selling my artwork wasn't even a dream on the horizon. I just wanted something meaningful that I could give to friends, and I also really enjoyed the soothing repetition of painting lines, loops, and words. So I wrote out grocery lists, inspiring quotes, the alphabet, and song lyrics. I practiced while on work phone calls, while watching TV, and while hanging out with my siblings. Finally, the lettering began to make sense and flow smoothly onto my paper. If you're in the very beginning stages of learning to letter, here are the exact, basic skills I learned that eventually led me to become a professional artist.

Practice the Downstroke

The very first thing I learned about lettering is that the downstroke is generally thick, and the upstroke is generally thin. This means that every time I draw a letter, the line that moves from top to bottom is wider than the line that moves from bottom to top. Before I had the right tools, I taught myself a sort of faux calligraphy with a Sharpie marker by drawing a double line for every downstroke and then filling it in.

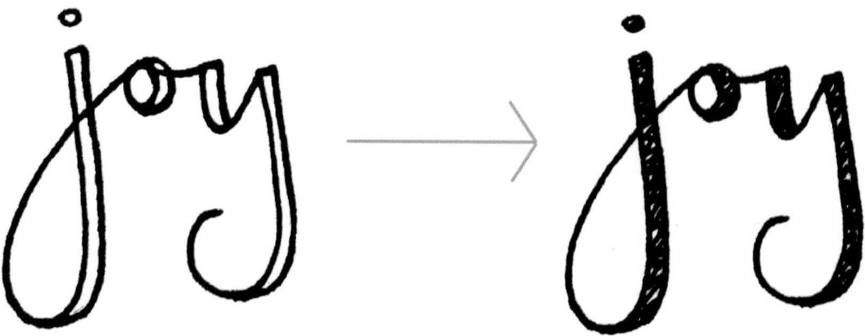

It took a lot of effort to make all the lines look uniform and smooth, so eventually I graduated to purchasing my first brush pen, and I've never looked back.

If you are using a brush pen or paintbrush, making a thicker downstroke means that you press slightly harder on the brush every time you move from top to bottom, and you take the weight of your hand off the brush every time you move from bottom to top. You want the upstroke to be thin enough that there's an obvious contrast to the thick downstroke. When you're first getting started, a good upstroke will feel like your brush is barely touching the page.

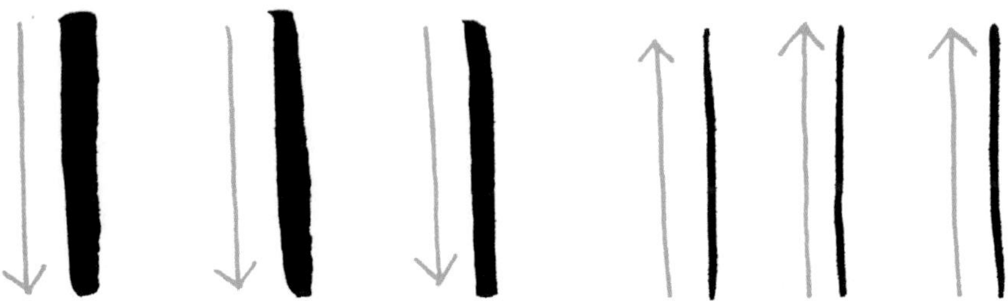

TIP: If you're working with a Pentel brush pen, squeeze the barrel gently until the brush is saturated with ink. If you squeeze too hard, ink will drop out onto your page, and your brush will be so wet that it will be impossible to create a thin upstroke. If you do happen to squeeze too much ink out, blot the brush on a paper towel until the ink is manageable on your practice paper.

In order to get familiar with the downstroke, I devoted many scratch pages to practicing zigzags and circles. I highly recommend that you put on a movie, grab your sketch pad and brush pen, and do the same thing! By practicing shapes and lines, you'll build muscle memory about thick and thin strokes so that you don't have to think about them when painting actual words. In the beginning, your lines might look shaky, rigid, or crooked. Don't feel discouraged. Eventually, your mind and hands will work together to create smooth, flowing lines.

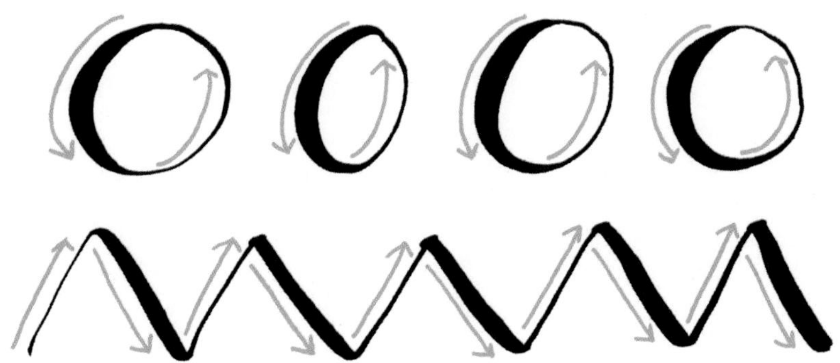

One of the most important habits to form while practicing shapes is keeping the angle of your lines consistent. When you eventually write actual words, you want the angles of your letters to be uniform in order to create an organized, readable page.

In addition to lines and circles, one of the primary shapes you'll form when writing letters are ascender and descender loops. Ascender loops are the tall loops on letters such as *h*, *l*, *f*, and *b*. Descender loops are the low loops on letters such as *g*, *j*, *q*, and *y*. Don't worry about writing full letters yet. For now, just build muscle memory in your hand as you practice thick downstroke and thin upstroke loops.

For ascender loops, use your lightest touch to draw a long upward angle to the right, then begin to add pressure to thicken the line as you curve left, and maintain pressure into your straight downstroke. Notice that the upstroke is angled and the downstroke is vertical. This combination helps the letter look clean.

For descender loops, begin with a straight, thick downstroke, then lessen pressure as you hook your brush to the left, lifting the pressure as you angle up.

Forming Letters and Words

Now that you've practiced brushstrokes, zigzags, circles, angles, and loops, you're ready to write letters! This next section might take you back to kindergarten, when you relied on lines that showed you how tall, short, and wide to make your alphabet. Eventually, you'll move on from this sort of structure in order to develop your own style; however, in the beginning, it's important to study basic letter proportions.

The four primary lines I use in lettering are the baseline, midline, descender line, and ascender line:

BASELINE: The line where all of the letters "sit."

MIDLINE: The line that marks the height of all lowercase letters that don't have an ascender (*x*, *o*, *m*, *n*, etc.).

ASCENDER LINE: The line that marks the height for letters that rise above the midline (*h*, *f*, *b*, etc.). I also use this as the line that marks the height for capital (uppercase) letters.

DESCENDER LINE: The line that marks the length of letters that drop below the midline (*q*, *g*, *j*, *y*, etc.).

A B C D E

F G H I J

K L M N O

P Q R S T

U V W X Y Z

a b c d e f

g h i j k l m

n o p q r s t

u v w x y z

CONFESSION TIME

In the first few months of teaching myself lettering, I relied completely on tracing other fonts. I didn't know what kind of style would feel comfortable or come naturally, and my hand still didn't quite understand how to form pretty lines. The easiest way for me to practice was to open up a Word document, type the alphabet in a couple of different fonts, print it out, and then trace them with my pencil. Afterward, I used my brush pen to go over my pencil lines. Eventually, these various fonts grew familiar enough to me that I didn't need to trace them anymore, and I ended up combining elements of different fonts into a new style that I could specifically call my own.

After you get the hang of writing your alphabet with standard proportions, it's time to begin finding your own style. There are countless ways to add personality to your words, and so my greatest (and most fun) advice is to experiment! Throw perfectionism out the window as you press your brush hard and soft on the page, practicing with big and small loops, various angles, flourishes, and fonts. Enjoy the messes and don't try to impress anyone; the more you let yourself experiment, the better you'll learn what types of letters come naturally to you. Then, focus on that style and develop it. Here are a few of the variations I use when designing a piece:

HOORAY

All uppercase letters

hooray

No loops on ascender or descender

hooray

Extended ascender and descender

hooray

Thin downstroke lines

Simple Pen Lettering

Sometimes I'm in the mood for my verses to have a simpler look, especially if the artwork surrounding the verse is particularly busy. In these times, I'll use my Micron pens instead of a brush pen to write out basic cursive words. I generally draw out the same fonts as the alphabets shown above because my hands are already familiar with the letter formations. However, on the uppercase letters, I'll add a few more fancy curves in order to elevate them to more than just plain cursive.

> With simple pen lettering, it can be easy to feel like we're in second grade, practicing our cursive handwriting. One ironic thing about me becoming a professional calligrapher is that my actual handwriting is terrible! If I begin my pieces with the mindset that I'm writing something, my letters turn sloppy. However, if I change my mindset to *drawing* the letters, they immediately look better. It's magic!

A B C D E

F G H I J

K L M N O

P Q R S T

U V W X Y Z

a b c d e f

g h i j k l m

n o p q r s t

u v w x y z

Choosing a Verse Layout

Whenever I'm lettering a new verse, the part of the process that takes me the longest is figuring out how to fit all the words together in a logical and appealing way. I'll frequently go through several sketches before I decide on my final verse layout. It's taken me tons of trial and error, but here's the method I've come up with.

- Write the verse on a scratch piece of paper and underline the words you want to emphasize. Take a look at your verse. Are there specific words that stand out? You could put these words alone on a line, make them bigger, or use a different font in order to highlight them.
- Decide whether you want the verse to be landscape (horizontal) or portrait (vertical). I normally base this decision on the length of the words I want to emphasize. For example, in Psalm 139:14, "I praise You, for I am fearfully and wonderfully made," the words "fearfully" and "wonderfully" are long and would look scrunched up if I tried to fit them in a portrait orientation. With Bible journaling, you'll usually need to go with a portrait orientation because the margins of the Bible are tall and skinny. However, if you feel like your verse will only look right if it's drawn in a landscape position, simply turn your Bible sideways and draw out the verse in the length of the margin.
- Sketch out the verse MANY times until you find a layout that (a) looks right, (b) has line breaks in places that make sense, and (c) has a style that fits the tone of the verse. Questions to ask: Is your layout balanced and even on both sides of the page, or does it look too heavy in a specific place? Does your placement of the words allow the verse to read logically, or are your lines broken up in a way that makes it confusing? Is your writing too fancy or plain for the specific verse you've chosen?
- Pay attention to negative space. Negative space is all the space on your paper that has nothing on it. It includes the margins of your page and the empty places between your letters and words. In my opinion, the use of negative space is one of the most obvious factors that sets apart an amateur and a seasoned artist. Specifics to look for: Are your words centered on the page, or is there extra negative space on the left side, right side, top, or bottom? Is your verse too big on the page, making everything look scrunched? Is the space between your lines and words consistent, or do you have some words packed together and some words floating alone? Are there any "holes" in the verse where you could exaggerate an ascender, descender, or another letter to even out the space?

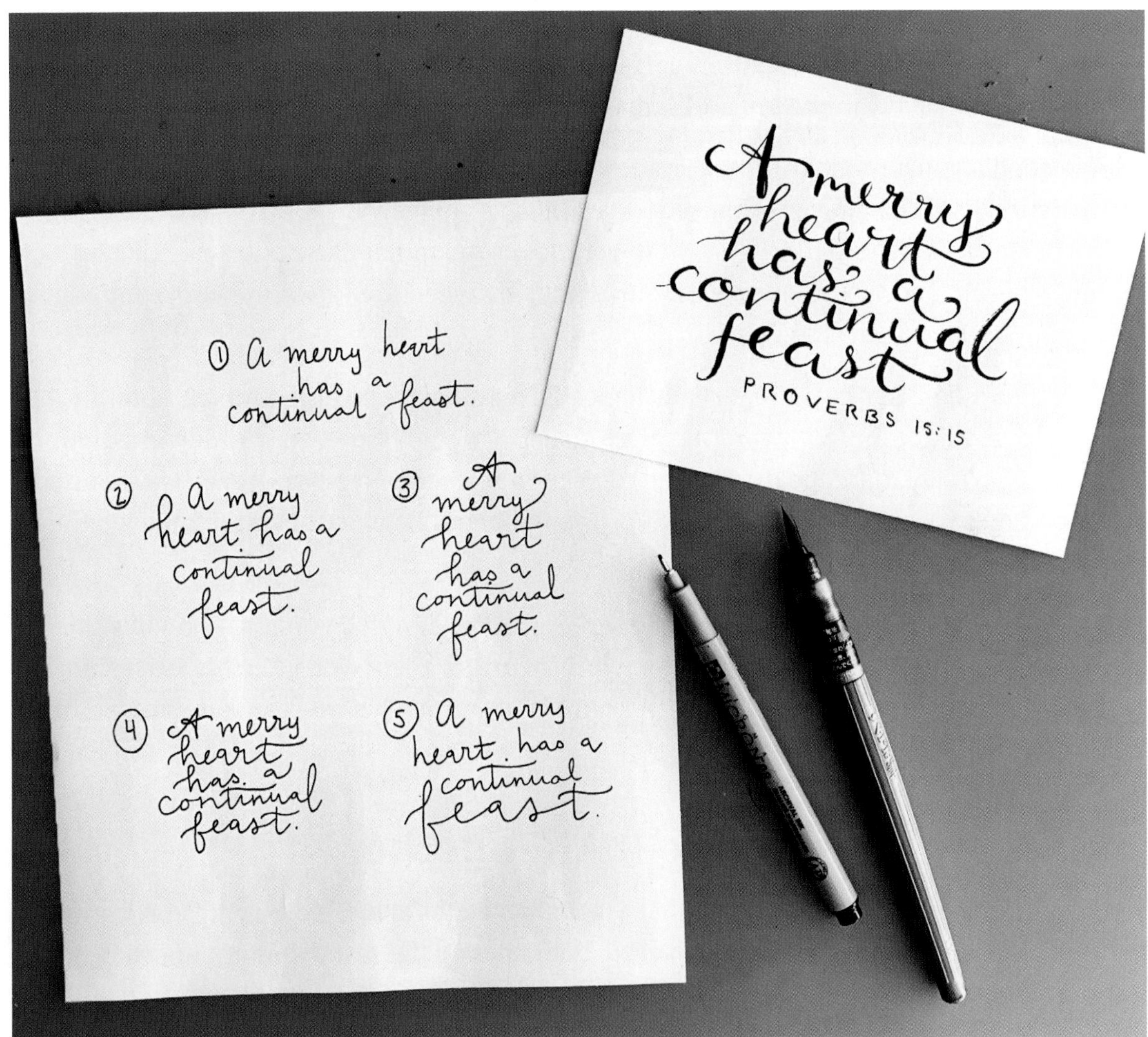

In this example from Proverbs 15:15, you can see that I sketched out five different verse layouts with a pen before deciding on the final version, which is written with a brush pen. (Full disclaimer: I usually do about twelve sketches before making a final decision!) As you can see, I decided to go with my fourth sketch. Here's why:

1. While this version feels balanced, it doesn't seem to carry enough punch on the word "feast." I decided that "feast" needs to be on its own line in order to better emphasize it. Also, notice that there is quite a bit of negative space on the second line ("has a"), but because it's equal on the right and left sides, it still makes sense.

2. This version seems to be making an upside-down triangle. The second, third, and fourth lines decrease in length in perfect diagonal lines toward the bottom, which makes it feel heavy at the top and unbalanced at the bottom.

3. I decided against number three for a few reasons. With each word on a separate line, it reads much slower because it takes the eyes longer to get through it. Also, the particular font I chose for the "A" at the top looks too much like a star when it's on a line by itself, and the difference in line lengths between the top of the verse and the bottom of the verse is too drastic.

4. I liked number four because it reads logically, feels balanced at the top and bottom, and doesn't have any awkward negative space. My only issue was that I wanted this piece to go in a landscape (horizontal) direction instead of a portrait (vertical) one, so when I drew it out for the final product, I lengthened the words and then placed the lines closely on top of one another.

5. While I like that the word "feast" is better emphasized in this version, I feel like the words aren't broken up logically. The word "heart" is a key word for this verse, but it's on the same line as "has a," which aren't key words. This makes it feel slower and more confusing to read.

Putting It All Together

It's time to put together everything that we've learned! Take a look at these two sample verses. Both are from the book of Proverbs, both take up the same amount of space on the page, and both are written with my brush pen. However, each verse has its own style. In Proverbs 16:32, I don't have any loops on the ascenders, and the letters are straight instead of angled. There is more negative space between the words, and all of the words are the same size. This simplicity helps it read a bit more straightforward and fits the masculine tone of the verse.

In contrast, Proverbs 31:25 has exaggerated ascender and descender loops, and the letters have a curvy, feminine feel to them. There is little negative space between words and lines, and specific words are larger (notice the difference between the words "and she" and "laughs").

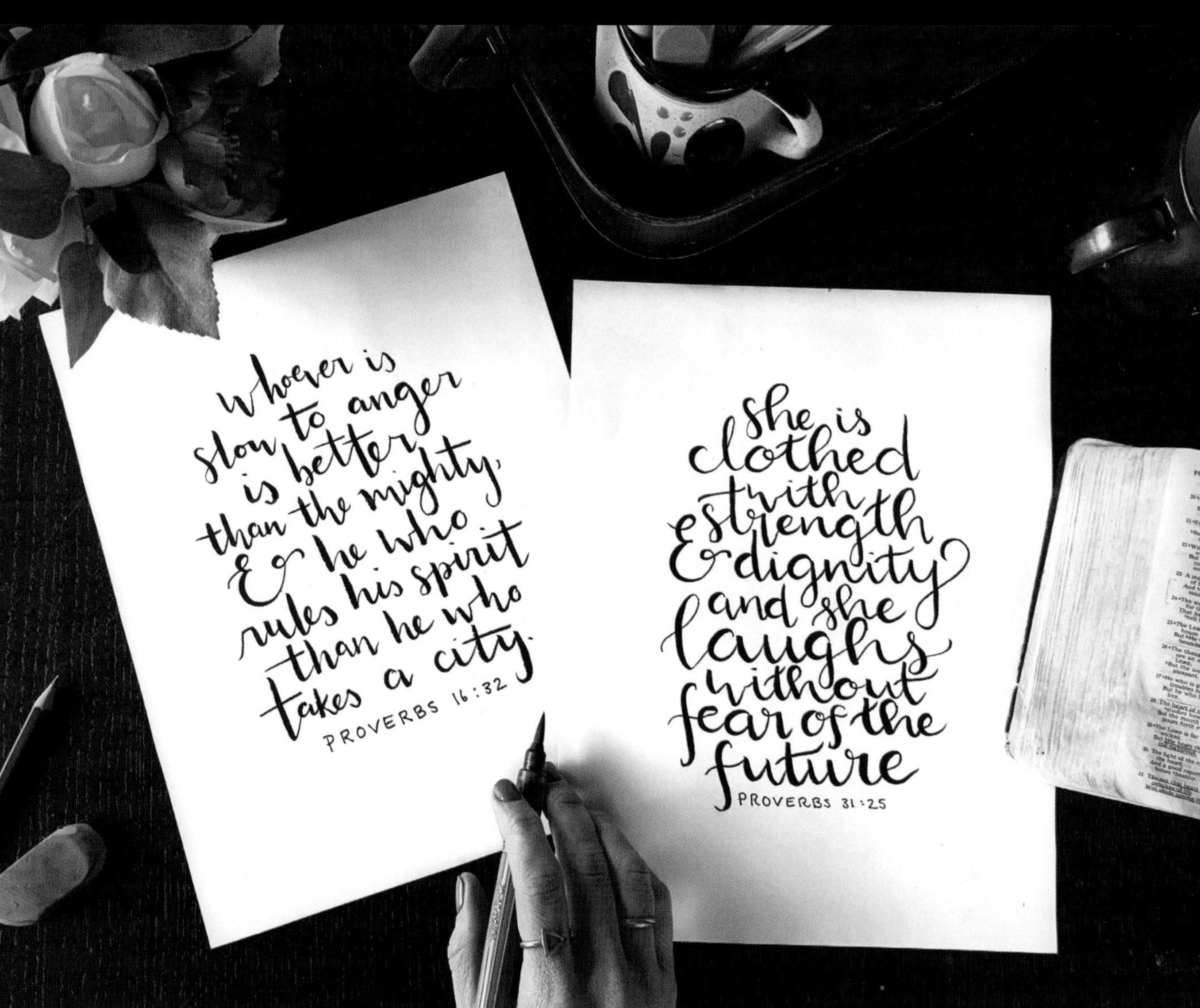

There are also some stylistic similarities between the verses. Both begin with a shorter line at the top, widen their lines in the body, and end with the shorter verse reference at the bottom. This helps the verse seem balanced and centered on the page, with evenly weighted negative space. Both verses also have a simple text print for the verse reference, which helps to set it apart and make the page a little more interesting.

Learning to letter and developing your own style is a soothing, beautiful hobby. Let yourself experiment, make mistakes, and draw out the same verse 100 times (great for Bible memorization!). Make sure you keep some of your initial work—when you look back after a few months of practice, you'll be amazed at how far you've come.

Chapter Four

INTRODUCTION TO BASIC WATERCOLOR

A few years into writing and selling my lettering online, I made Mother's Day cards for my mom, grandmother, and older sister. The Scripture verses on the front of the cards felt empty without any border design, and I felt a sudden urge to teach myself watercolor flowers. So I took the same approach I used with brush lettering: I watched some YouTube videos, got out some paper and a paintbrush, put on a movie, and started practicing. The first several pages went straight into the trash—all of my colors ran into each other, turned brown, and couldn't hold any sort of form. But eventually, through experimenting with different ratios of paint to water, color mixing, zigzags, and circles, I figured out how to paint.

Before you get into any of my watercolor recommendations, my hope is that you'll experiment on your own first. Reading a thousand books on painting is no substitute for actually picking up your brush, putting it to paper, and practicing. So, before you move forward, grab your paints and begin to play. Feel curiosity surge through your fingers as you enjoy watercolor without trying to master any techniques. What happens when you use hardly any water? What happens when your brush and paints are completely soaked? What's the texture difference when you drag your brush versus when you roll your brush down the page? Do you prefer starting with wet paper or dry paper? What sort of depth do your colors have if you let them dry before adding a new layer? Does the depth change if you add layers while your first colors are still wet? Everything you read in the rest of this chapter will make more sense if you've first filled up a few pages with your own experiments.

I'm absolutely crazy about every ounce of texture that watercolor brings to the page. Do you have blooms of color that burst outside of their spaces and into other shapes? Perfect. Hard lines layered over soft fades? Gorgeous. Come to terms with the fact that watercolor has a brilliant mind of its own. You will make mistakes, throw away tons of first drafts, and get better every day, but your painting journey will be much more enjoyable if you give yourself grace to play and experiment.

Now that you've had some fun, let's move on to a few painting exercises. But first, a big disclaimer: because I have zero formal training in art, the following instructions might break all sorts of official painting rules. (For example, I hardly ever use watercolor paper. While the rough, toothy grip of watercolor paper helps the paint feel manageable and stay in place, I just love the way the colors mix on a smooth page.) In fact, the times I've read watercolor blogs or books, my mind has wandered because I've felt lost among the specialized vocabulary and lengthy explanations. The following strokes, strategies, and skills are the ones that have made the most sense to me, and I hope they'll be helpful to you too. Ready to break some rules?

Lines

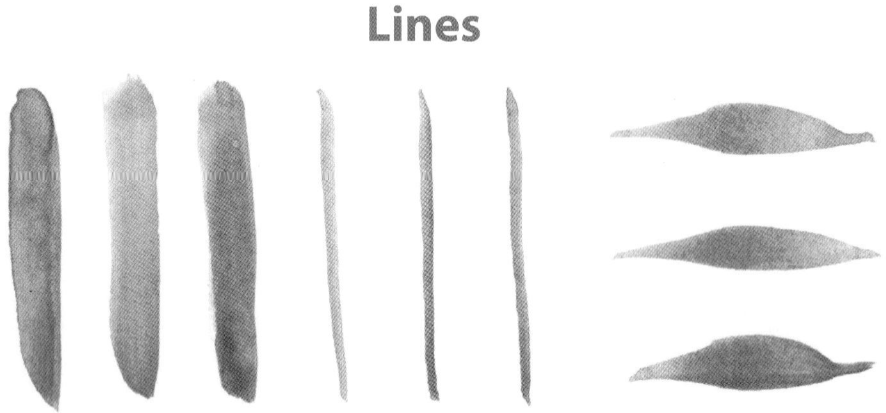

Dip a round brush (I'm using a Pentel water brush, but any medium-sized round brush will do) in clean water and load it up with paint. Practice brushing straight, thick lines by pressing the belly (the biggest part) of your brush onto the page and dragging it down. Vary the thickness of your lines by increasing or decreasing your hand's pressure on the brush. Next, practice thin lines by placing just the tip of your brush on the page and gently pulling it down. Be careful not to add pressure as you move so that your line will stay the same width.

After getting the hang of thick and thin lines, try a combo! Begin by placing just the tip of your brush on the page, then press the belly of your brush onto the page as you paint a horizontal stroke, ending by lifting it back up to just the tip. This sort of brushstroke is how I paint leaves in my floral paintings.

Saturated to Transparent Colors

One rule of watercolor painting that I fully agree with is using water to lighten a color instead of mixing in white. When white combines with other watercolors, it turns them a bit muddy and hinders lovely transparent textures from showing up. For this exercise, we will practice making colors lighter and darker by using just water and a single paint color.

Roll your round brush in paint until it's fully coated with color, and then paint a small, square swatch. You want this square to be the full, exact paint color you see in your pan or tube, and so saturated that the color won't change if you add more paint to it. Next, dip your brush in a glass of water and then tap the excess water off on the rim of the glass. You've just decreased the amount of paint on your brush by washing a little bit off in your water glass. Paint another square swatch, and you'll notice that this time the color is slightly lighter. Meanwhile, the water in your glass will take on more of the paint color. Dip your brush back into the water, tap off the excess, and paint another square. Repeat this process until the paint on your brush is completely diluted, and the square you paint is purely the color of your tinted water.

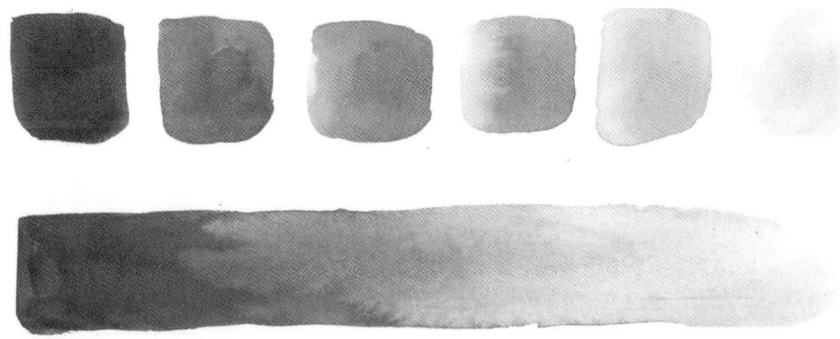

Next, practice going from saturated to transparent in one full fade. You will use the same lightening technique, but this time you'll join the squares together, blending the two with your brush. Often, I find that the amount of water on the page seems overwhelming, so I'll blot my paintbrush onto a paper towel in order to remove a bit of color and water in between squares (more on this technique, called lifting, later; see page 38). Don't worry if there are a few hard lines between your colors. These will improve with practice, and they're also quite beautiful!

Circles: Understanding a Source of Light

This exercise hits on two important skills: painting round strokes to form a circle and designating the source of light. Look at the balls below, and pretend a flashlight is shining on them. In the first ball, the flashlight is shining on the top right, and the ball grows gradually darker toward the bottom left. In the second ball, the flashlight is shining in the middle, and the ball gets darker in a circle around the light. In the third ball, the flashlight is shining on the bottom left. This sort of shading helps an object appear to lift off the page, adding dimension where it once looked flat. After I realized the difference a unified light source can make in a picture, I began to prioritize it in my paintings. This is especially true if I'm painting a more complicated image with various shapes and angles.

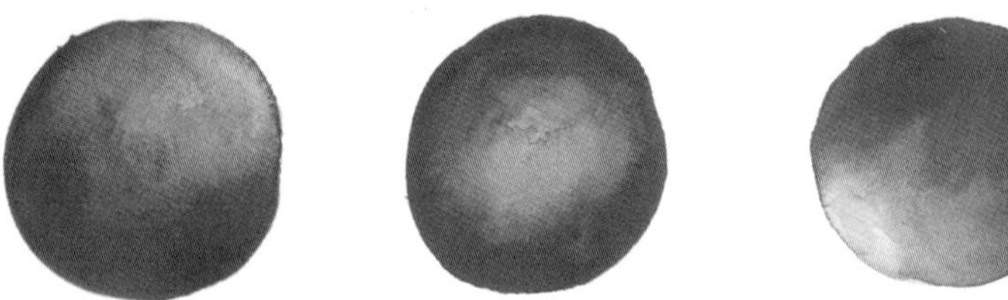

For example, this is a wishing well that I painted for my sister. Notice how my light source is coming from the right side, causing the stones, bucket, wood, and beams to all have lighter tones on the right and darker tones on the left. By keeping the light source the same for all these elements of the painting, the wishing well feels harmonious and full.

Practice source-of-light shading with watercolors by using the same technique as your swatch exercise above (see Saturated to Transparent Colors, page 34). Pretend that a flashlight is shining down from the top right of your page. Roll your round brush in a color and paint a large, tilted *C* shape, with the opening of the *C* facing the top right corner. Then dip your brush in clean water, tap off the excess, and paint a smaller *C* directly inside the first *C*. Lighten your color again and paint an even smaller, nearly closed *C* inside the last one. By now your nested *C* shapes should be starting to form one big circle. Continue working inward, removing paint from your brush until you have a round ball with your darkest color at the bottom left and your lightest shade at the top right.

TIP: When the bristles on a paintbrush fan out, they'll leave individual, disjointed lines on the page. If this happens, either rewet your brush with paint or water, or gently rotate your brush on the paper until all the bristles taper into each other again.

Blending Colors

Hooray! You're becoming a total pro at lightening, darkening, and blending watercolor paint. Your next step? Adding a second color into the mix! For this exercise, we'll practice the transition from dark blue to dark green.

Fully coat your brush in dark blue, paint your first swatch, and then lighten the next two swatches a bit more drastically than you did with the one-color exercise (see Saturated to Transparent Colors on page 34). Next, clean your brush in fresh water, load it with green paint, and then move a few spaces over to paint a dark green swatch. Head back toward the center as you lighten two green shades, meeting the light blue square in the middle.

Now, practice painting a continuous rectangle blend of blue to green. Begin with blue, lighten to the middle, then pick up your brush, clean it in fresh water, and move it right to paint the dark green. Lighten the green as you head center again. When the two light colors meet in the middle, your rectangle might feel like it's overflowing with water. Below, you'll learn about a technique called "lifting," which is how I remove the excess water from my painting.

Lifting Paint

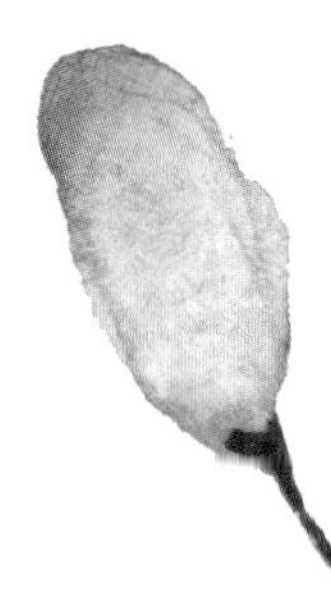

Sometimes I realize that I've used too much dark paint over an area that should be light, and I want to "erase" a section. Lifting paint is a gorgeous way to remove some color and blend the area into surrounding shades. One way to lift is to simply dab excess wet paint with a paper towel, but I find this creates harsh separation between the space I'm trying to remove and the nearby colors (also, small fibers from the paper towel are sometimes left behind). Instead, I like to soak my brush with clear water and gently touch the area where I want to remove color. Then, I lightly dry my brush on a paper towel and return to the wet page, soaking back up the water that has now mixed with the color from my painting. I repeat this process of blotting my brush on my paper towel and then soaking up the paint and water until I've removed as much color as I can.

After practicing this technique a few times, I realized that I love the look of this lifting effect even when I'm not trying to remove color. I purposefully lift paint in order to create smooth leaves, diffused edges, and perfectly blended complementary colors. For example, the image above depicts a leaf from a Sedum Aurora, a succulent plant whose leaves are a lovely translucent combination of pink and green. My original leaf (on the left) looked too saturated and heavy. Lifting the paint allowed the colors to fade into each other with a more transparent texture.

Paint Wash

One of the most simple and stunning ways to combine watercolor with lettering is to paint a wash background, let it dry, and then write over it with either a brush pen or a Micron pen. Washes are perfect for Bible journaling because they're one of the only ways to add color to an entire page and still read every single word of text.

Painting a wash is similar to painting the long rectangles in the blending exercises above. Beginning with the color of your choice, coat your brush in paint and make a broad horizontal stroke. Next, dip your brush in water, tap off the excess, and make another, lighter horizontal stroke directly below (and flush with) the first one. As you make this stroke, the paint from the first line will bleed into this second one, but you might have to go back with your brush to better blend the two hues together. Many times washes have a pretty, ombré effect, but there are no rules! Feel free to re-saturate your brush in paint again, adding darker areas in the corners or letting the texture of the water take on a life of its own. The only factor you want to keep in mind is to make the wash light enough that your future writing will show up on top.

Let your wash completely dry and then use your brush pen or Micron pen to write a Scripture verse on top of it. I recommend first choosing your verse layout and doing a practice run on a different piece of paper—I've fallen in love with a wash only to realize that I had no actual plan for the look of my verse once I started writing it out. By conceptualizing your verse on another sheet of paper first, you set yourself up for success when combining your two elements.

ACRYLIC PAINT

While watercolor is my main jam, I'll turn to acrylic paints every once in a while if I'm in the mood to create something a bit bolder and brighter. Acrylic paints offer a striking, smooth contrast to a watercolor aesthetic, and I love using them when I want to create areas of flat, opaque color instead of blended layers. Get familiar with your acrylics by painting simple, square swatches. I recommend lightly dipping your brush in water to begin because it slightly thins the paint and makes it smoother, but you don't need to wet your paints or use water throughout your painting process (apart from cleaning your brush between colors).

A second difference between acrylics and watercolor is that lighter acrylic colors can easily be layered on top of darker colors, as long as the first layer of paint is completely dry. This is helpful when you're painting something with a dark background.

A Note on Colors

Choosing a color palette for a painting is one of the most important parts of the process, and while you can find endless opinions in books and online, color combinations are some of my favorite rules to break! Yes, it's true that the colors you choose will totally change the look of your picture, which is exactly why you should go with colors that you love and that make you feel happy when you see them together.

The best way to get inspired for a color palette is to walk outside. Nature is the ultimate teacher, and we have brilliant color-combination examples in every terrain. If I'm hoping for a soft aesthetic, I might look up photos of the desert, where muted green cacti grow out of tan sand and rocky maroon mountains fade in the background. This completely contrasts with the electric feel I get from looking at ocean images, where neon yellow fish swim in navy blue waters, vibrant orange coral underneath them. The color palette changes again with the cool blues and deep greens of the forest, and yet again with the striking purples, reds, and pinks you'll find in a sunset. Decide on the general mood you desire for your painting, and then find colors that fit that mood in nature and in your mind.

Chapter Five

FLOWERS AND BORDERS

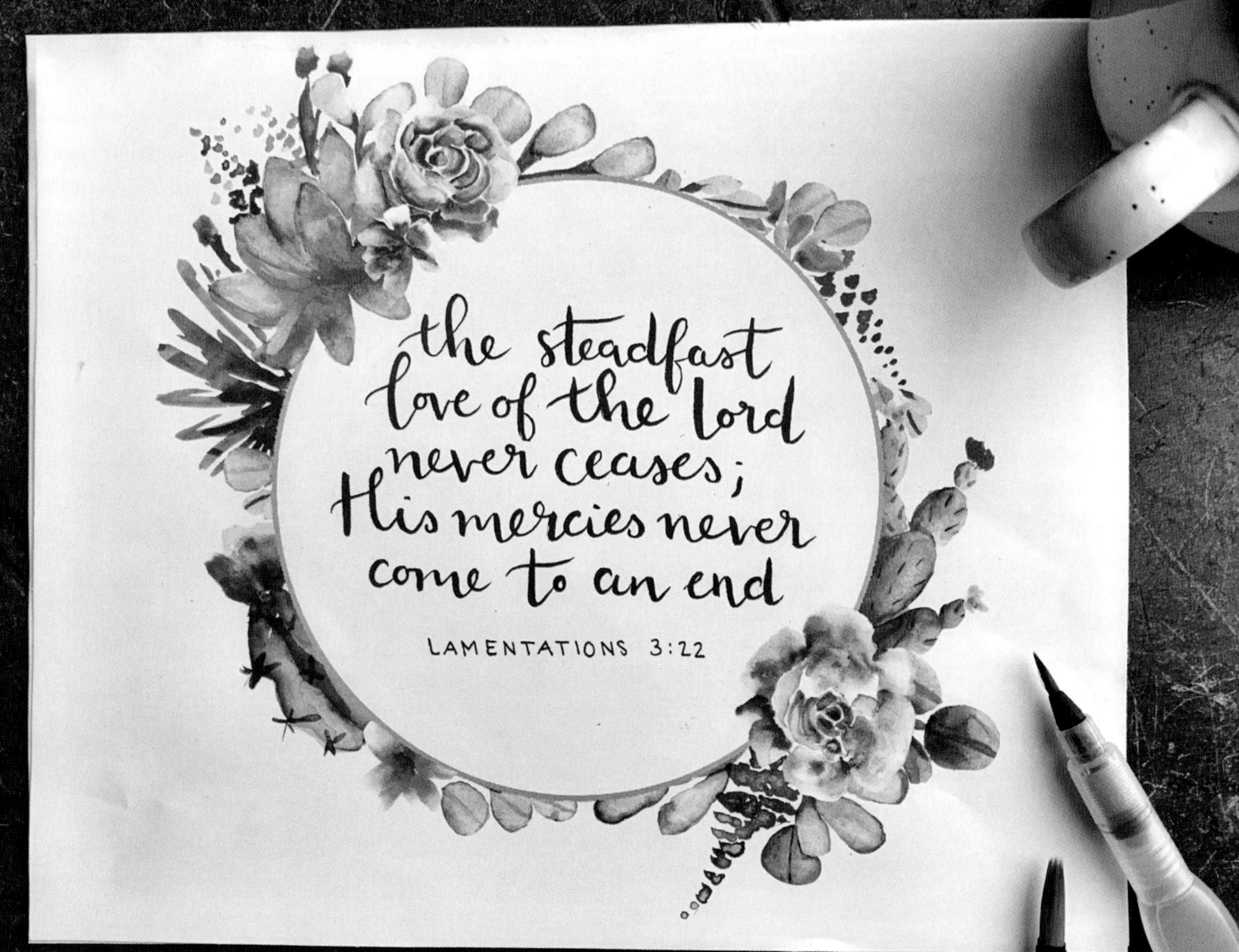

We've gotten to my favorite part! I have painted and drawn countless watercolor flowers, and I don't think I'll ever get tired of them. As you learn these techniques, remind yourself that your picture shouldn't necessarily look like mine. Just as every flower in the entire world is unique, you will never be able to paint the same flower twice. It's part of the beauty and magic of illustrating nature, and it also frees us from stressing out about getting our picture exactly right.

Painting Watercolor Flowers

To begin, let's practice concentrating color at the tip of our brush. With watercolor, when you lift your brush off the paper at the end of a stroke, you normally leave behind a saturated spot of color. For this flower technique, we want to learn how to push that color toward the center of the flower.

Wet your brush and swirl it in blue paint. Touch the tip of your brush to the page, and then flatten out the belly of your brush to the side. Don't drag your brush at all. Instead, simply lift your brush back up to your starting point, and then take it off the page. You should have a single dab of blue, with the majority of the color concentrated at the tip.

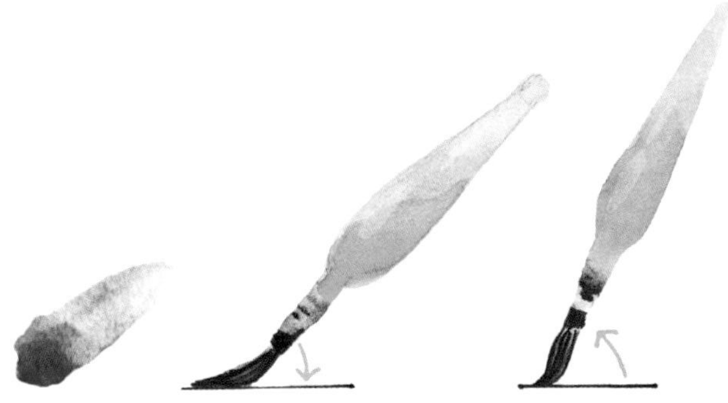

Swirl your brush in blue paint again. This time touch the tip of your brush to the page and flatten out the belly, but instead of lifting it back up to the starting point, roll your brush in a downward curve. I literally twist the barrel of the brush between my fingers, causing the brush to do a full 180° roll in my hand as the wet bristles roll on the page. Make sure to keep the tip of the brush generally in the same place and just curve the outer edge of the brush

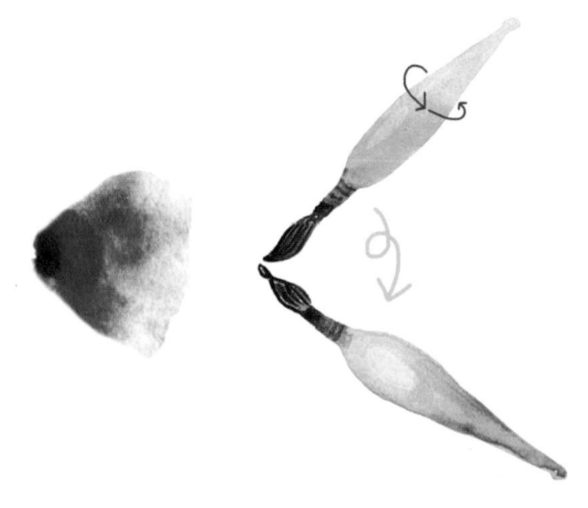

down, making a sideways triangle petal shape. Then, lift your brush back to the starting point, leaving the full concentration of blue in the base of the flower petal.

Now, either angle your brush to make more petals in different directions, or just rotate your page.

Practice adding a different number of petals to your flower. To paint only a few petals, you want to roll your brush in a wider curve. To paint many petals, roll your brush a shorter distance. Don't worry if your petals are slightly different sizes. This is normal for any flower!

Now, take a look at the dimension you add when you swirl just the tip of your blue-coated brush into some black paint. Following the above steps, press the belly of your brush onto your page, rotate in a downward curve, and then lift your brush back up to the tip. By painting with two colors at one time, you'll add a rich complexity to the flower that you otherwise won't see by layering colors on top of each other at different times. Your next step? Play around with all sorts of color combinations. My favorites are a red brush with a purple tip, a pink brush with a maroon tip, and a purple brush with a black tip.

A beautiful way to add interest to your watercolor piece is to paint flowers facing in different directions. To begin, load up your brush with blue paint, then dip the tip into a dark purple. Roll your brush down to create your initial petal. Now, reload your brush with color, place the tip above your initial petal's starting point, and drag your brush a short distance at an upward angle until you get to the top of the initial petal. Here, press the belly of your brush down and roll your brush about a third of the distance of your first petal. (Note: This roll is slightly different than your previous twists because you are not keeping the tip at the same place and making a triangle. Instead, you are rolling the full brush—tip included—down the page.)

Next, reload your brush with color and roll it down along another third of the initial petal. Paint the final petal by rolling along the last third of the initial petal and then dragging the brush to the starting point of that petal. Finish the flower by cleaning your brush, dipping it in green, and painting the stem.

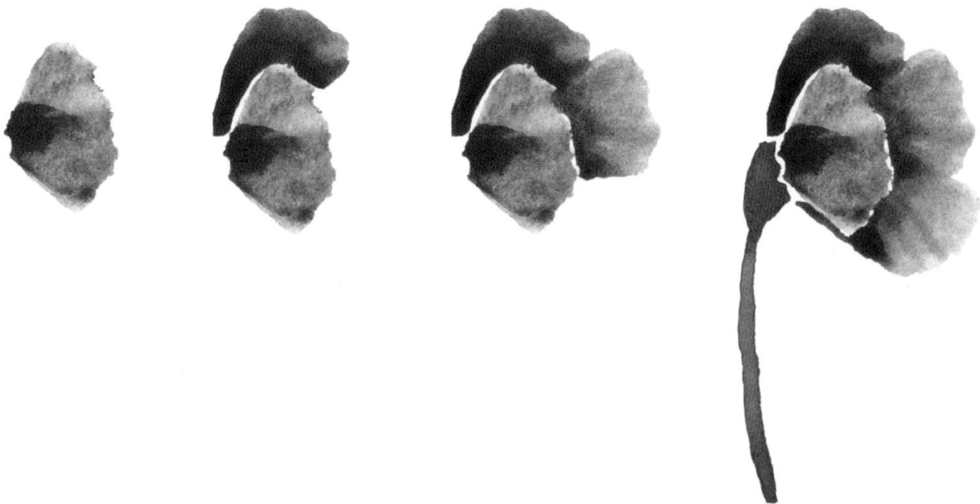

Once you feel comfortable with simple forward- and side-facing flowers, challenge yourself to add a bit more complexity. Begin with the center of your flower and move outward. After your initial petals are painted, add the next layer of petals around them. For now, continue to concentrate color toward the center of your flower in order to create contrast between petals.

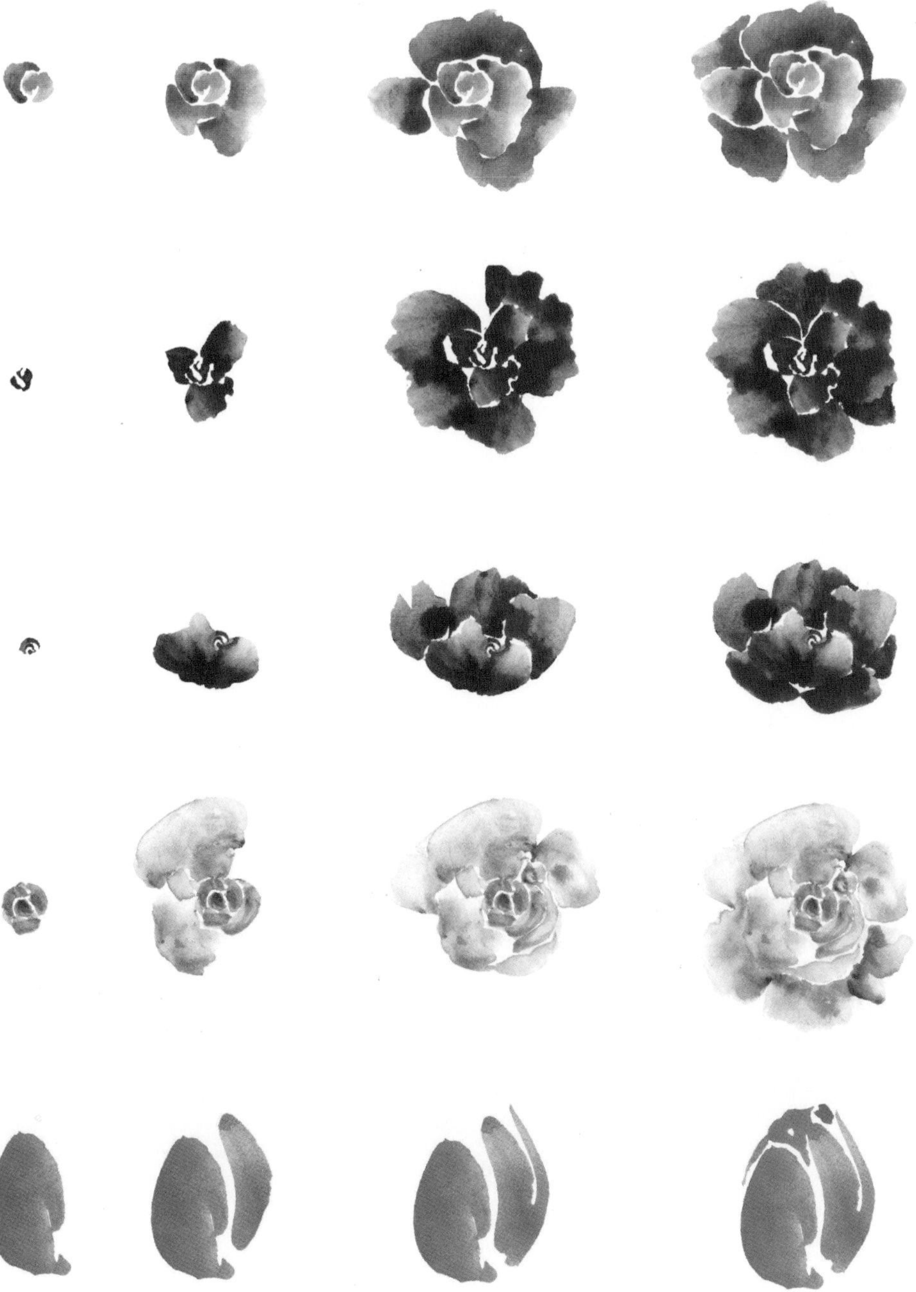

May the God of hope
fill you with all joy & peace
as you trust in Him, so that
you may overflow with hope
by the power of the Holy Spirit.

ROMANS 15:13

When painting a floral bouquet or border with watercolors, I lightly sketch out placement of my flowers and leaves with a pencil first so I know where I want everything to go. This helps me take into account some of the elements we talked about in Chapter 3, such as negative space. I want my flowers to look balanced on the page, and an initial sketch helps me make sure there aren't any gaping holes where I need to adjust the size of my flowers or add some extra leaves. Once I start painting, I begin with the lightest colors first (if I try to layer them on later, they won't show up). After painting the lighter colors, I go back through and add darker florals and leaves, and I finish with whatever verse I want to include with the painting.

Drawing Flowers with Pens

Every once in a while, I get into a watercolor rut. Rather than trying to force myself forward, my best bet is to take a break, get my creative juices flowing, and try another medium. When this happens, I like to totally change up the look of my picture, and I go for an option that's both more striking and simpler: pen florals.

Thin-lined flowers are a gorgeous way to add a modern, feminine aesthetic to your Bible-journaling pages. Because Micron pens work well on thin paper and the flowers are so simple, they work perfectly as borders and illustrations. The primary skill needed to draw pen florals is an eye that can pull basic shapes from a real (or fake) flower. For this exercise, I purchased a simple bouquet from my grocery store, but it's just as easy to look up your favorite flower online and go from there. Remember that your flowers will look different than mine, and that's great! No two flowers are the same, so feel confident when your lines vary from the instructions I've outlined below.

To begin, scan your flower for the most obvious shapes you can pull out, such as wavy triangle petals, oval flower buds, and linear stamens. For this first poppy, draw one simple petal. Next, draw a slightly shorter petal coming out of the middle of the first petal. Then, add two long petals, one on each side. Finally, finish with the stamens in the middle and a curve on the inside of a petal to add dimension.

This second flower is similar to the daisies you've probably doodled before. To begin, draw one petal, and then add a few more. (Tip: Your flower will look more realistic if you make the ends of your petals wavy.) To finish, add some stamens in the middle and lines on the inside of a few of your petals to give the look of them curving in.

This third flower is a little more complicated, because we've changed our angle and added a second layer of petals facing different directions. To begin, draw two petals that are short and wide. Next, draw stamens in the middle and then two smaller petals behind them. Third, draw petals all around your initial layer. Notice that the petals on the bottom have a sort of flat edge, and that they still seem to come out of the center of the flower. Finally, add lines on the inside of a few of your petals so they look like they're curved.

Finally, the rose! (I always have difficulty with roses, no matter how many times I draw or paint them. If your brain struggles to grasp these lines, you're not alone.) To begin, draw a swirl for the center and a line coming down. This is the center of the rose. Next, add some wavy lines that curve around the center, staying open at the bottom. Third, anchor your wavy lines with vertical lines, and at the bottom of these lines draw a long horizontal line to begin a larger petal. Fourth, draw two lines below to make a curvy *V* shape to create the body of the rose, and draw one large curve on top to start the background petals. Fifth, form the outer edges of the *V* with wavy lines coming out of the body of the rose. Notice that the top parts of these lines are horizontal and flat, and then they wave down to connect to the bottom of the *V*. Finally, draw some triangular and flat petals around the outside of the flower, and draw one flat petal at the bottom to add dimension.

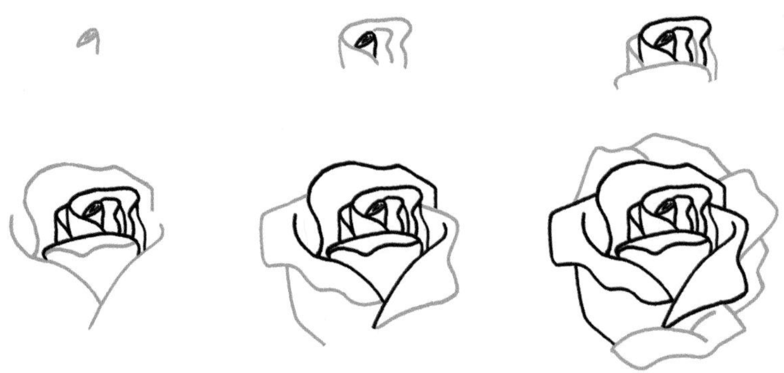

Painting Flowers with Acrylic Paints

Acrylic paints are another way to totally change the look of your flowers, turning them into bold, fun elements that pop off the page. To paint acrylic flowers, I first sketch out a simple line flower like the ones we practiced drawing above. Then I paint each petal individually. Subtle brushstrokes help differentiate each petal, letting our eyes make better sense of the flower. If I've drawn out curves along the edge of any petals to add dimension, I use a slightly darker shade to color them in.

In the painting below, you can see a few of the ways I vary my acrylics. In the first flower, my pen strokes underneath the paint are visible, helping differentiate the petals from each other. In the second flower, there are no visible pen strokes. In the third and fourth flowers, I've painted the flower and then redrawn over my pen strokes with an 08 Micron pen. This gives the flowers a bright, defined look.

You're ready to go wild, child! Play around with your paints and pens as much as you possibly can. Take them with you to school, doodle with them when you're daydreaming, keep them handy in your car and while you're on the phone and when you're hanging out with family. Let illustration be a new avenue to see this brilliant, bold world with fresh eyes and an imaginative mind.

Borders, Banners, and More

I love using flags and ribbon banners in Bible journaling to highlight something specific, like the theme of a verse or a word that stands out. Likewise, borders are an easy way to give a page definition, helping my journaling look put together and finished. Borders are also a way to separate different thoughts I have for various verses on the same page.

To draw flag banners, simply make a curved line between two upper corners of your page (as if it's a string that's tacked up at both ends), and then draw a series of evenly spaced flags hanging from it. The flags can be any shape you like. I usually put a bit of distance between my flags because it helps them look simpler.

The secret to drawing ribbon banners is to make sure that all of your parallel lines are exact copies of each other. As you can see from the examples, I always begin with the body of the banner, drawing two parallel horizontal lines. Then, I connect the horizontal lines together with vertical lines at each end to form a curvy rectangle, and I finish by adding the folds and background of the ribbon. Make sure that the ribbon backgrounds are always the same width as the main body of the ribbon.

To draw a border, simply use your ruler to make a straight line, and then add a pattern of shapes along that line. There are an infinite number of variations you could make; decide how complicated or simple you'd like your border to be, and then leave space between your shapes accordingly.

Chapter Six

LET'S TALK ABOUT PERFECTIONISM

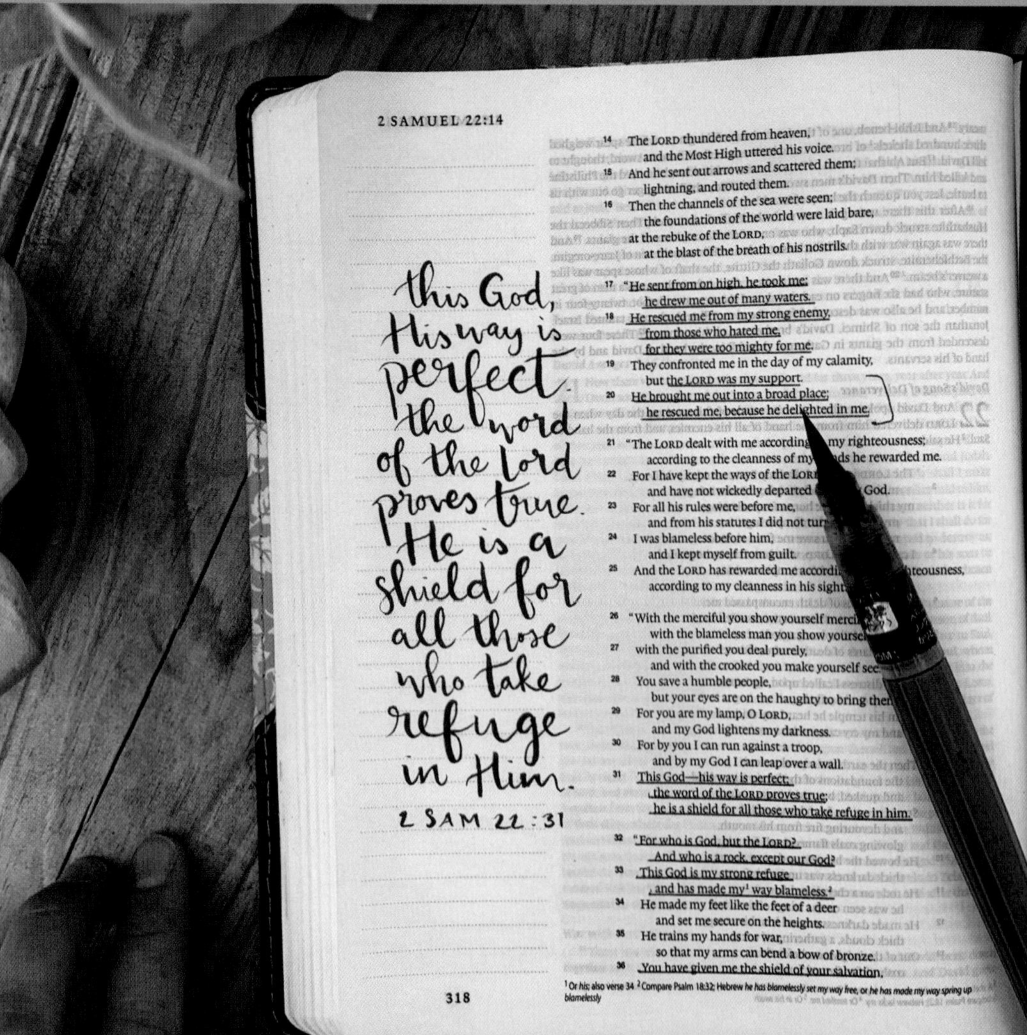

Sister, it's the moment we've been waiting for! We've covered tools and history, lettering and illustration. Now it's time to actually begin journaling in our Bibles! Open up those crisp, pristine pages, grab your paintbrush, and . . . feel a bit nervous? Yeah, me too.

When I first started this process, Bible journaling sounded great in theory but totally scary in practice. The pages of my Bible were immaculate, untouched, and clean. I felt comfortable underlining beloved verses, but the thought that I would mess up the page with bad paintings, smudged calligraphy, or wobbly words was enough to stop me before I ever started. Basically, I felt like if the page wasn't perfect, it was a failure.

What Is Perfectionism?

Perfectionism (noun): a personal standard, attitude, or philosophy that demands perfection and rejects anything less.

I remember the first time somebody called me a perfectionist in college. They didn't mean it as a compliment, and I was so frazzled by their negative assessment of me that I went on a journey to find the perfect way to overcome perfectionism. (Cue the facepalm emoji.) I figured that if I could just find a step-by-step guide, I'd follow the directions to a T and come out on the other side more relaxed and carefree. I also figured that the Bible had something to say about it, but when I looked up the word "perfect" in my Bible app, I felt more discouraged than ever. What was I supposed to do with a verse like "You therefore must be perfect, as your heavenly Father is perfect" (Matthew 5:48)?

But I also knew something else about God, and it drove me to keep studying and asking for wisdom to understand hard passages. I remembered Romans 8:1, which says, "There is therefore now no condemnation for those who are in Christ Jesus." Perfectionism always left me feeling condemned (guilty, disapproved, unfit), but this verse said that that feeling wasn't from God. In fact, when I looked at the context of the verse (reading the surrounding verses to understand what the author was saying to the original readers), I discovered that this entire section of Romans has a lot to do with perfectionism. Paul is distraught because he wants to perfectly follow God's law, but he's totally incapable of it. A few verses earlier, he says, "I have the desire to do what is right, but not the ability to carry it out" (Romans 7:18). Ugh. Guilty. Disapproved. Unfit. So how did Paul come to the conclusion that he shouldn't feel condemnation? He realized that he was in Christ Jesus.

Friend, this is the gospel message. God is entirely perfect and entirely whole. You and I, no matter how hard we try, have broken God's law (sinned) and fallen short of that perfection. But God, rich in mercy and full of love, sent His perfect Son to take the consequence for our sins. It's the great exchange: on the cross, Jesus traded His perfect life for all of our mistakes. The Bible says that He became our sin so that we could become the righteousness of God. Did you catch that? If you have repented (turned) from your sin and placed your faith in Jesus, it means that you are in Christ, and there is therefore now no condemnation on your life. When God looks at you, He sees the perfection of Jesus.

Perfectionism is normally rooted in both a desire for approval and a fear of failure. But in Christ, we are already approved by God. And in Christ, all we do is win, because He has already had the victory over every single failure. My friend, perfectionism no longer needs to have a hold on our lives. Our approval is based not on our perfection for Jesus but on Jesus's perfection for us.

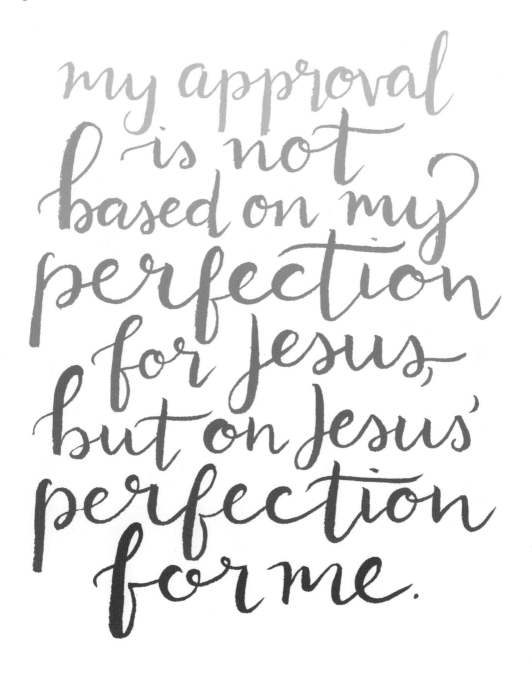

my approval is not based on my perfection for Jesus, but on Jesus' perfection for me.

So what does this mean for you and I as we get started with Bible journaling? Perfectionism can be a total pitfall to stop us from ever trying. Celebrating the perfection of Jesus, however, can fuel inside of us a holy curiosity about the Word of God. When we use Bible journaling as an opportunity to be a student of Scripture instead of an opportunity to display our own creative masterpieces, it gives us freedom to throw off perfectionism and replace it with worship. We aren't working for Instagram likes. We aren't stressing about whether our lettering is "good enough." Our eyes are on God's majesty instead of our own artwork, and there's something more important than the fear of making mistakes: painting God's word becomes worship, and knowing Jesus becomes the prize. Let God's glory take center stage in your heart, and use the margins of your Bible to investigate, grow, and love the Perfect One.

In order to settle these things in my heart, I decided to write my very own permission slip right in the beginning of my journaling Bible. On the Old Testament introduction page, I drew a huge scroll and granted myself permission to make mistakes.

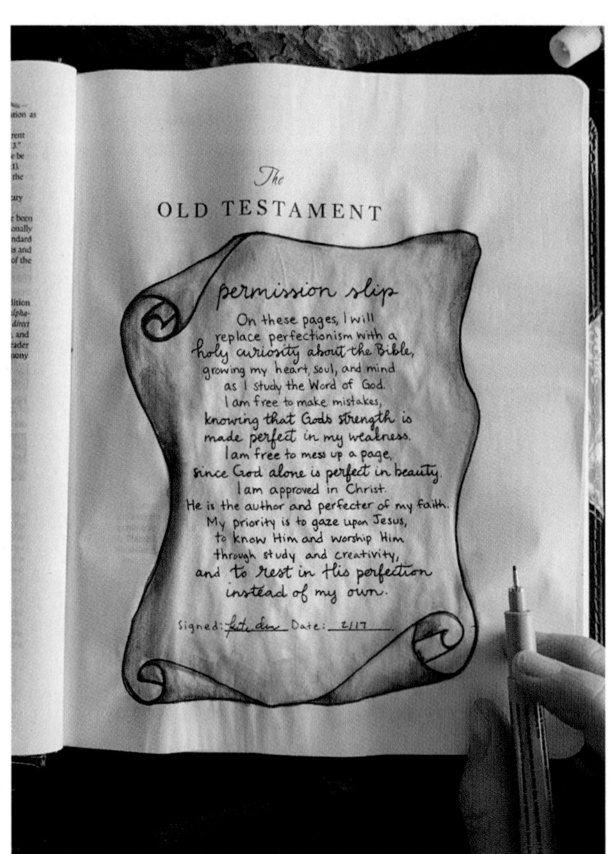

In case you need the same sort of internal agreement, consider writing something similar in the beginning of your own Bible. It is your official permission slip. You are free to turn your eyes away from yourself and toward the perfect Christ.

SECTION 2

Bible journaling strategies

Chapter Seven

SCRIPTURE MEDITATION AND MEMORIZATION

When I was ten years old, I was homeschooled alongside my brother and sisters, and my mom had us all memorize Psalm 91 as part of our daily curriculum. At the time, the chapter seemed to be eternally long, and each of the sixteen verses felt irrelevant to my ten-year-old problems. But my lifelong, insatiable commitment to winning fueled competition in me toward my siblings, and I memorized that chapter word for word.

Fast-forward twenty years, to when I was in the middle of writing this book. In early 2020, the coronavirus pandemic hit the United States. Hospitals were quickly overrun, and the country was effectively shut down to prevent the spread of the disease, leaving countless without jobs. Within a few months millions of Americans had been infected, and more than a hundred thousand had died.

While sheltering at home with my husband and two-year-old son, I felt anxiety hovering hour by hour, as terrifying news saturated every conversation and social media post. The economy looked grim, and I felt scared for my family and friends. But in the middle of all the noise, a phrase kept rising to the surface of my heart: "He will command His angels concerning you, to guard you in all your ways." It's Psalm 91:11, and it appears among three other verses that specifically talk about deadly disease. I used to know these verses as head-knowledge, but now, suddenly, they'd become heart-knowledge too. Soul-knowledge. God is Emmanuel, God-With-Us, even in the face of a global pandemic. He commands His angels concerning us. He is our refuge and fortress, our God, in whom we trust. I drew out Psalm 91 on a huge sheet of paper and added color around the corners, meditating on each word. I hung up these treasured verses for me and my family to see every day, helping us align our minds to the truth of God's word. Peace rules in our hearts and in our home.

Why Should We Memorize the Bible?

Memorizing for the Long Run

I didn't know it when I was a ten-year-old girl, but memorizing Psalm 91 was like a spiritual investment. Normally when someone is making a financial investment, they put money into an account that they don't benefit from immediately. The money stays there for a while and grows, especially if more is added to it. It provides the owner with confidence, security through life's ups and downs, and is extremely helpful if an emergency suddenly arises.

Memorizing Psalm 91 is an investment I made as a little girl that will pay off for the rest of my life. And it's defining moments like the coronavirus pandemic that have made Scripture memory a consistent priority for me throughout the last twenty years: I memorize for my current self, but I also memorize as an investment for my future self. I have no idea what beautiful or painful circumstances I will someday face, but in the middle of a crisis, I don't want to find that my internal spiritual account is empty, desperate to be filled with emergency deposits from the opinions of other people, news headlines, or an endless scroll of digital distractions. Instead, I want my heart, soul, and mind to pull from an account rich in the Word of God. I want to be filled to overflowing with hope, wisdom, strength, and truth for the journey.

Memorizing to Form Our Lives

Apart from spiritual investments, why do we memorize the Bible? It's not so that we can show off impressive knowledge, win a trophy in Bible trivia, or debate people who think differently than us. Memorizing the Bible is not as much about gaining information as it is about the formation of our lives. We write verses on our hearts and minds in order to form our understanding of God, form our character, and form our emotions, responses, attitudes, and loves. As we etch passages of Scripture into the grooves of our minds, the sacred words take root inside of us, changing us from the inside out. They turn into patience with our siblings, groceries for the homeless, hatred of racism, and friendship extended to the girl who sits alone. The memorized word shows up in world-changing justice, such as the fight against human trafficking, and in heart-changing service, such as doing the dishes without being asked. Deuteronomy 30:14 says that the word is "in our mouths and our hearts so that we can do it." The Bible is not just a book to be read; it is a book to be lived.

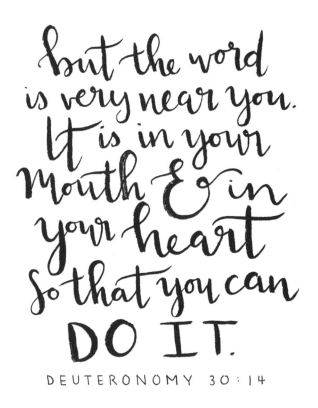

> but the word is very near you. It is in your Mouth & in your heart so that you can DO IT.
>
> DEUTERONOMY 30:14

He who dwells in the shelter of the Most High
will REST in the shadow of the Almighty.
I will say of the Lord, "He is my refuge & my
fortress, my God, in whom I trust." Surely He will
save you from the fowler's snare, & from the
deadly pestilence. He will cover you with His
feathers, & under His wings you will find
refuge. His faithfulness will be your
shield & rampart. You will not fear the
terror of night, nor the arrow that flies by
day, nor the pestilence that stalks in the
darkness, nor the plague that destroys at midday.
A thousand may fall at your side, ten thousand
at your right hand, but it will not come near you.
You will only observe with your eyes & see the
punishment of the wicked. Because you
have made the Lord your dwelling place—the
Most High, who is my refuge—no evil
shall be allowed to befall you, no plague come
near your tent. For He will command His angels
concerning you, to guard you in all your ways.
On their hands they will bear you up, lest you strike
your foot against a stone. You will tread on the
lion & the adder; the young lion & the serpent
you will trample underfoot. Because he holds
fast to Me in love, I will deliver him. I will
protect Him because he knows My name. When
he calls to Me, I will answer him. I will be
with him in trouble. I will rescue him &
honor him. With long life I will satisfy him
& show him My salvation. -Psalm 91

Memorizing for Nonstop Access to the Bible

A third reason to memorize the Bible is that it gives us 24/7 access to the very words of God. After I got my first iPhone, I stopped reading and memorizing the Bible as intentionally because I felt like it wasn't as necessary. It seemed like I didn't need to put in the difficult work of memorization if I could just look up a verse at any moment of my day.

I realized pretty quickly, however, that this wasn't the case. In the middle of an emotional conversation with a friend, it didn't feel good to push the pause button as she poured out her heart so that I could type the right phrase into Google to look for a verse. No, I wanted the Word of God inside me, able to be ushered out at that very moment to provide hope and counsel and comfort for her. Similarly, I've been unbelievably grateful for memorized verses in these first two years of motherhood. Crinkly Bible pages are an incredible temptation for a baby, and it's hard to sit down for a solid amount of time to read without him needing something. But the Bible is with me. I access it while I'm driving, while I'm laying my son down to sleep at night, and while we take walks around the neighborhood. I'm not dependent on convenient timing. At any moment of my day, I can meditate on Scripture because it's already in my mind.

Bible Memorization Strategies

Now that we've talked about the why, let's get to the how! I've found that the best way for me to memorize Scripture is to combine the three strategies listed below.

1) Repeatedly say the verses out loud
2) Meditate on meaning
3) Draw it out

Repeatedly Say the Verses Out Loud

While researchers disagree on the exact number of times it takes to memorize something by saying it aloud, most of them say that it's well over 20 times, and many say it needs to be read aloud between 50 and 100 times! At first these numbers felt daunting to me, but after putting this into practice, it's become one of the best habits of my life. I could say the same passage a thousand times out loud and still find that the living and active Word of God is teaching me new truths about His character and our world.

Meditate on Meaning

Nowadays the word "meditation" is widely associated with practices like yoga and mindfulness, but the Bible talks about a different sort of meditation. Instead of focusing on our breath or emptying out our mind, Christian meditation involves actively filling our minds with Scripture.

After reading a passage aloud several times to begin memorizing it, I start truly meditating on the various words in the passage. For example, the first verse of Psalm 91 is "He who dwells in the shelter of the Most High will rest in the shadow of the Almighty." In meditating on this verse, I asked myself a series of questions: What does it mean to dwell in God's shelter? How can I practically apply this to my life? Am I currently dwelling under the covering of something else, like anxiety or fear? What would it mean to dwell under God's covering instead?

Another key aspect of meditating on a verse is reading it in the context of the surrounding verses. Sometimes we hear a famous verse that seems inspirational, only to find out later that the actual meaning of that verse is completely different than we thought. As Christians who are basing our lives on the Word of God, it is crucial that we take time to learn what God is actually saying.

A small example of this is Psalm 46:5, which says, "God is within her; she will not fall." This verse is written in beautiful calligraphy all over Pinterest, mass-produced on journal covers, and printed on the back of girls' soccer team jerseys. However, if you read the rest of Psalm 46, you'll find that the "her" in the verse is actually referring to the "city of God," or the church as a whole. It's important to know this, because the truth is that you and I *will* fall at various points throughout our lives. If we think this verse means we should expect to succeed at every turn, we might become angry with God when it doesn't come true, thinking that He didn't fulfill His promise to us. When we realize, however, that the collective church of God will always remain, it can produce a different type of worship inside of us.

Psalm 46:5 is still a great verse to memorize. God will always protect the great work of love and redemption He is doing through His church on earth. We can have confidence that even if we mess up, or our youth pastor or Sunday school teacher messes up, God's church stands strong. God is within her; she will not fall.

Draw It Out

You've probably heard it a thousand times: if you want to remember something, write it down! And it's for a good reason: different parts of our brain process different types of information, and writing something down activates multiple regions at the same time. It takes significantly more time to draw out a word than to read it, say it, or type it, and so constructing each word means that you are coding it into your brain on a deeper level. For this very reason, I never mind drawing out dozens of "rough drafts" of Bible art before I get to the final version. I know that each time I mess up and start over, I'm giving myself another chance to truly digest the words I'm trying to memorize.

For this project, I chose to memorize Jeremiah 17:7–8. Its tree metaphor is such powerful imagery, and I knew that it would be fun to paint. To begin, I sketched out the tree and leaves with a mechanical pencil, being careful to not press too hard. Then, I placed a thin cardboard sheet underneath the page to ensure that nothing would bleed through onto other pages. I traced my pencil marks with a black Micron 05 pen (but used a thinner 01 pen for the trunk, since I knew I'd be painting words on top of it) and then gently erased the pencil marks underneath. For color, I used a small, round brush to paint the leaves with

acrylic paint in three shades of green (Light Green, a mixture of Light Green and Phthalo Green, and a mixture of Light Green and Yellow Medium). The acrylic paint covered up quite a bit of my Micron pen marks, so I retraced them once my paint dried. Finally, I wrote out the verses with a black Micron 01 pen, tracing over some of the downstrokes with the faux calligraphy technique to make them stand out.

Scripture Memory Page

Memorizing Bible verses can sound great in theory, but unless we actually commit to the process and do the hard work of turning it into a habit, it's easy to forget and eventually give up. I generally discourage a checklist mentality when it comes to the Bible (time with God shouldn't just be a task we check off our to-do list), but I've found that having a weekly plan helps me stay consistent.

When I got my journaling Bible, I decided that I wanted to try memorizing something every week. One way of keeping myself accountable was to create this Scripture Memory Page, which I drew on the inside of my Bible's back cover. I made fifty-two little checkboxes, one for each week of the year, so that I could track my progress. There are a couple of options when creating a page like this, and both options are a great choice. It just depends on what works best for your brain and your schedule.

OPTION 1: Decide which verse you'd like to memorize at the start of every week and write it on the checklist then. While it would seem ideal to memorize something from a passage you're currently reading, this won't always line up. Some books of the Bible will take you several weeks to get through, with only one or two verses you'd memorize word for word (think Old Testament genealogies or long stories), and some books of the Bible will take you a single day to read, but you'll want to memorize the entire thing (I feel this way about many New Testament letters). If you choose this method, I recommend just picking a verse you love every week, whether it's from your current reading location or not, and sticking to it.

OPTION 2: Decide which verses you'd like to memorize at the start of the year and write down all of the references at one time. This is the method I chose because I can be a pretty indecisive person. I knew that if I was choosing a new verse each week, I'd spend way too much time trying to find the "perfect" verse rather than actually reading my Bible and working to memorize something.

To decide which verses to memorize, I flipped through previous sections I'd underlined and loved but not yet memorized word for word. If you don't have any verses underlined in your Bible, you can ask your pastor for verses he'd recommend, do a quick search online, or choose a book of the Bible and start reading through it for verses you'd like to memorize (I recommend Psalms, Proverbs, or any of the letters in the New Testament). Some of my choices are single verses, and some are entire chapters. I know that throughout the year, my schedule will vary, with busy weeks and relaxed weeks. I don't plan on going in order for all of these verses; if I have a busy week, I'll look through my list and choose a short verse to memorize. If I have a more relaxed week, I'll choose a longer passage.

For this project, you'll need:

- Ruler
- Pencil
- Eraser
- Two different-colored highlighters (I chose pink and orange)
- Micron 05 and 01 pens

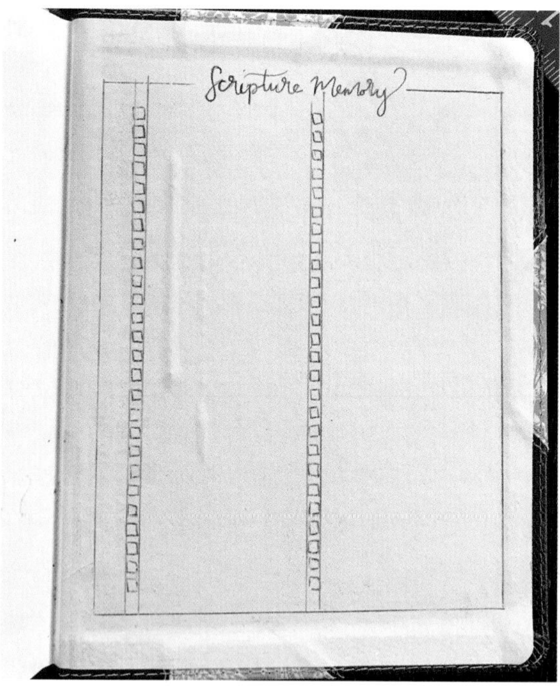

1. To begin, use a pencil and ruler to draw a rectangle along the border of your page, leaving a small opening at the top to write the header "Scripture Memory." Next, take your ruler and draw two vertical parallel lines close to the left border, and two vertical parallel lines a little to the right of the center. These lines will be the left and right borders of your checkboxes, helping them to be uniform in size and location. Place the ruler near the top of the page and use it as a baseline for the squares, moving it slowly down the page and drawing the squares on top. In total, draw fifty-two little checkboxes (twenty-six in each column).

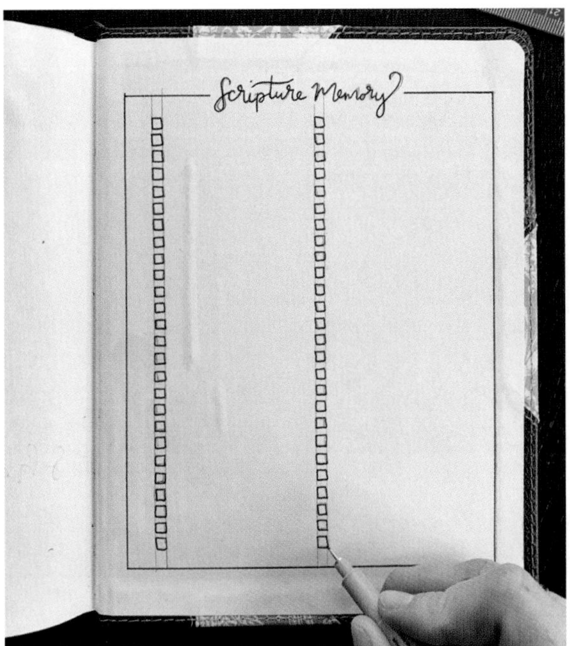

2. Trace over all of your pencil marks with a Micron 05 pen, using a ruler to keep the lines straight.

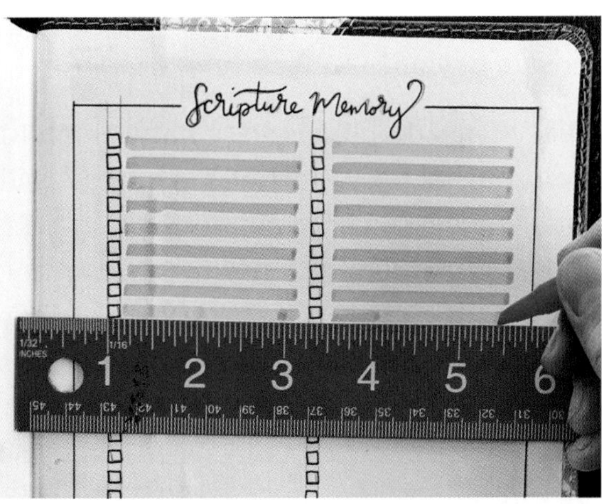

3. Place your ruler at the base of the top two boxes. Press the tip of your first-color highlighter (I used pink) to the ruler and draw a straight line across, breaking for the box in the middle. Then, move your ruler to the base of the two boxes below, and use your second-color highlighter (I used orange) to do the same. Repeat this process and pattern all the way to the bottom.

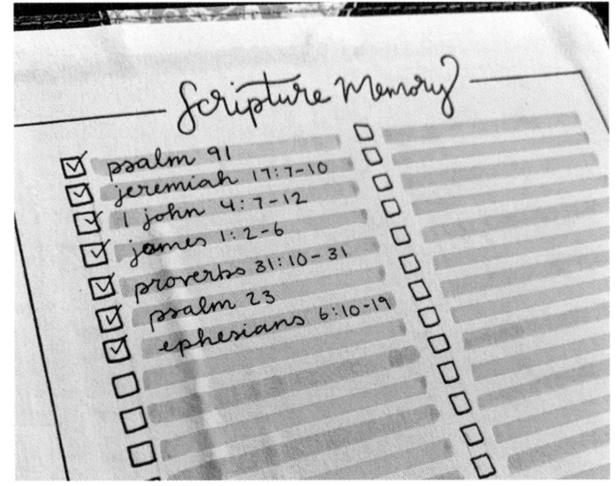

4. Gently erase all of your pencil marks. Using a Micron 01 pen, list the verse(s) you'd like to memorize each week.

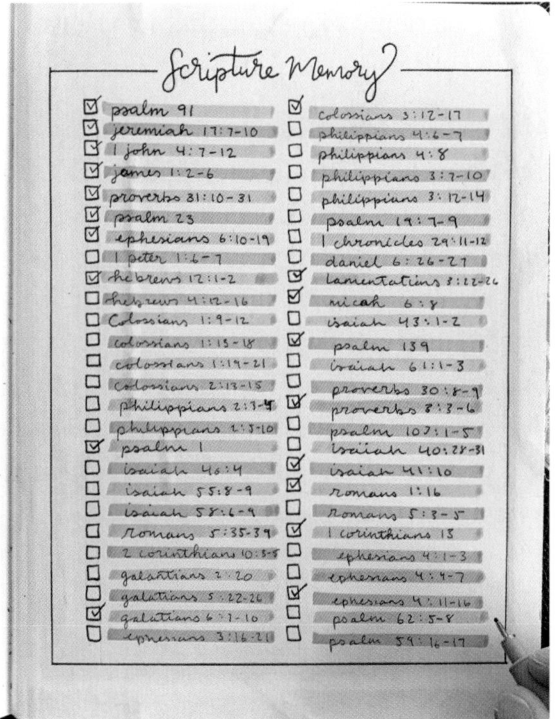

Chapter Eight

PRAYER JOURNALING

I remember being a little girl and getting my first diary, the heart-shaped lock and key ensuring that none of my siblings could read about my secret crushes. I loved to write, and I filled the pages with melodrama about every single thing. Yet it felt weird to send sentences into the blank abyss. I wanted to write *to* someone. I think I was around twelve years old when I realized that I could combine my deepening love for Jesus with my longing to constantly document my life. I could pray inside my journal.

At first, writing "Dear Lord" at the top of each diary page didn't feel very natural (and I always notice that if I take a long break from prayer journaling, restarting the process still feels a bit stiff). But the more I put pen to paper and let my heart pour out honest thoughts, the more I knew that prayer journaling was creating a special connection with God. Writing out my prayers gave me a focused space to dive deep with Him into specific areas of my life, helping my thoughts stay organized long enough to really process a situation. Issues that normally felt jumbled and confusing found new clarity as I worked through them with the help of God's wisdom and friendship. Something significant was taking place inside me as I processed my daily life—my insecurities, dreams, and romances—with God through writing to Him.

PSALM 38:9
O Lord, all my longing is before you;
my sighing is not hidden from you.
My heart throbs; my strength fails me,
and the light of my eyes—it also has gone from me.
My friends and companions stand aloof from my plague,
and my nearest kin stand far off.
Those who seek my life lay their snares;
those who seek my hurt speak of ruin
and meditate treachery all day long.
But I am like a deaf man; I do not hear,
like a mute man who does not open his mouth.
I have become like a man who does not hear,
and in whose mouth are no rebukes.
But for you, O LORD, do I wait;
it is you, O Lord my God, who will answer.
For I said, "Only let them not rejoice over me,
who boast against me when my foot slips!"
For I am ready to fall,
and my pain is ever before me.
I confess my iniquity;
I am sorry for my sin.
But my foes are vigorous, they are mighty,
and many are those who hate me wrongfully.
Those who render me evil for good
accuse me because I follow after good.
Do not forsake me, O LORD!
O my God, be not far from me!
Make haste to help me,
O Lord, my salvation!
What Is the Measure of My Days?
39
TO THE CHOIRMASTER: TO JEDUTHUN. A PSALM OF DAVID.
I said, "I will guard my ways,
that I may not sin with my tongue;
I will guard my mouth with a muzzle,
so long as the wicked are in my presence."
I was mute and silent;
I held my peace to no avail,
and my distress grew worse.
My heart became hot within me.
As I mused, the fire burned;
then I spoke with my tongue:
"O LORD, make me know my end
and what is the measure of my days;
let me know how fleeting I am!
Behold, you have made my days a few handbreadths,
and my lifetime is as nothing before you.
558
Lord,
the last few days have felt so overwhelming!! Being a mom while running a business while writing a book while being a wife all during quarantine. no childcare. no starbucks escape. no chance to escape with a friend. Also, what if we get really sick? What would we do with Cassius? Lord, what if our parents get sick? What if we couldn't say goodbye?
I'm tired. So tired. Tonight dan told me that I was "getting stuck" again, and it was sadly the perfect description. Just staring blankly while holding Cassius, who is struggling so much with his stomach, leaving me so helpless. Lord, I know that's for another time, but gosh, it's one of the hardest things right now. What do I do about Cash's tummy?
PSALM 40:6
Surely all mankind stands as a mere breath!
Surely a man goes about as a shadow!
Surely for nothing they are in turmoil;
man heaps up wealth and does not know who will gather!
"And now, O Lord, for what do I wait?
My hope is in you.
Deliver me from all my transgressions.
Do not make me the scorn of the fool!
I am mute; I do not open my mouth,
for it is you who have done it.
Remove your stroke from me;
I am spent by the hostility of your hand.
When you discipline a man
with rebukes for sin,
you consume like a moth what is dear to him;
surely all mankind is a mere breath!
"Hear my prayer, O LORD,
and give ear to my cry;
hold not your peace at my tears!
For I am a sojourner with you,
a guest, like all my fathers.
Look away from me, that I may smile again,
before I depart and am no more!"
My Help and My Deliverer
40
TO THE CHOIRMASTER. A PSALM OF DAVID.
I waited patiently for the LORD;
he inclined to me and heard my cry.
He drew me up from the pit of destruction,
out of the miry bog,
and set my feet upon a rock,
making my steps secure.
He put a new song in my mouth,
a song of praise to our God.
Many will see and fear,
and put their trust in the LORD.
Blessed is the man who makes
the LORD his trust,
who does not turn to the proud,
to those who go astray after a lie!
You have multiplied, O LORD my God,
your wondrous deeds and your thoughts toward us;
none can compare with you!
I will proclaim and tell of them,
yet they are more than can be told.
I need your help, Father. I need your help to WAKE UP to this current life, even in exhaustion, even in quarantine. Lord, I need you to meet me in this season. Inspire my heart. Wake up my body. Open my eyes to the incredible gifts all around me—my exceedingly thoughtful husband, who is growing your fruit every day, my joyful son, my home and delicious food and the opportunity to know you every day.
Lord, meet me in this season. I don't want it to be wasted. Pull me out of the miry clay, the clay of sluggishness, of stupor, of exhaustion & complaining, and envy and laziness. Help me to COME ALIVE with the beauty all around me. Let me share it with others. Let my heart sing a new song to you that would inspire others to sing. Lord, meet me in this season. I don't want to waste it.

Remembering God's Faithfulness

After a few years of prayer journaling, I realized that it was influencing my life in a different, powerful way. Every once in a while, I'd pick up one of my old prayer journals to read before going to sleep. As I flipped through the pages, remembering all the past hardships God helped me overcome, the truths He taught me, and the ways He answered my prayers, my faith grew for the trials I was currently facing. I had filled up books with evidence of the presence of God in my life, and reading through them served as energizing reminders of His faithfulness to me.

If we're not remembering, we're forgetting. We can have a thousand encounters with God—times He's provided for us, healed us, protected us, comforted us—and forget them all as soon as we look away. Scripture tells many stories of this happening even with our biblical heroes. For example, Aaron (Moses's brother) was completely involved with every single one of the plagues that hit Egypt. Since Moses had a speech impediment, Aaron was his spokesman and did all of the talking with Pharaoh. This means that Aaron saw the unmatched power of God in turning water to blood, parting the Red Sea, and more. Yet when Moses left the Israelites for a few days to get the Ten Commandments from God, Aaron was easily peer-pressured by the Israelites into making them a golden calf to worship. Even though Aaron repeatedly experienced firsthand the miraculous power of God in Egypt, he forgot about it once he got into the wilderness.

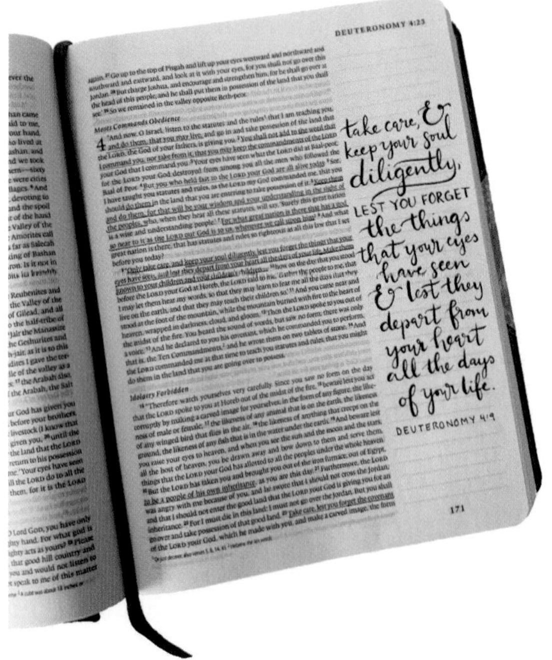

In the New Testament, we see another story about forgetting what God has just done. Mark 8 tells the story of how Jesus multiplied seven loaves of bread to feed four thousand people. Afterward, He and His disciples get on a boat to go to a new city, and the disciples think Jesus is upset with them because they didn't pack any bread to eat on their trip. Jesus responds, "Do you not remember? When I broke the five loaves for the five thousand . . . Also, when I broke the seven for the four thousand? . . . How do you not understand?" The disciples see Jesus provide more abundantly than they could have ever dreamed, and then, within the same breath of Scripture, they almost immediately forget that He can meet all their needs.

If we're not remembering, we're forgetting, and prayer journaling is a game-changing way to remember. Psalm 37:3 says, "Trust in the Lord and do good . . . feed on His faithfulness." By intentionally writing out the ways God is blessing me, helping me, and growing me, I am preparing a feast of God's faithfulness for my future soul. I know I'll face days where I feel empty inside, hungry for the approval of others, and exhausted from feeling like my life doesn't measure up. On those days, I can instead open up my prayer journals to an absolutely nourishing, filling table. I can feed on His faithfulness.

trust in the Lord
& do good;
dwell in the land
& feed on His
faithfulness.
PSALM 37:3

Why Do We Pray?

While you may be interested in using your journaling Bible for writing out prayers, it might feel uncomfortable if you've never really done this sort of thing before. Sometimes prayer gets categorized into super-specific moments in our lives—before meals, before bed, and at church—and it takes an intentional drive to push it past those boundaries. Yet in the Bible, we see constant evidence that God is fully relational, describing His love for us through the intimate metaphors of a father and son, bride and groom, artist and clay. There is a heartbreaking contrast between the thriving friendship God offers and the confining times of day in which we take Him up on all He has to give.

In the Old Testament, we see a relational God in the Garden of Eden, where God walked with Adam and Eve. We see a relational God in our understanding of the Trinity, where the Father, Son, and Holy Spirit are in perfect unity with each other. From shutting the door of Noah's ark with His very own hand to personally leading the Israelites out of Egypt, to expressing deep anguish when His people reject Him, we see that God is intricately involved in this world. Take a look at these verses from Psalm 139, where we get a glimpse of God's intimate knowledge of us:

O LORD, you have searched me and known me.

You know when I sit down and when I rise up;
you discern my thoughts from afar.

You search out my path and my lying down and
are acquainted with all my ways.

Even before a word is on my tongue, behold,
O LORD, you know it altogether.

You hem me in, behind and before, and lay your hand upon me.

Such knowledge is too wonderful for me; it is high; I cannot attain it.

Where shall I go from your Spirit? Or where
shall I flee from your presence?

If I ascend to heaven, you are there! If I make
my bed in Sheol, you are there!

(Psalm 139:1–8)

In the New Testament, God's intention for relationship with us explodes into shocking, radical depths. Scripture says that God so loved the world that He made the eternity-altering decision to send Jesus to earth, to have actual, tangible, in-person friendships with us, dying for us so that we can live with Him forever. Yes, God's intention for relationship went so far that He left the perfection of heaven, where there was never a bad smell, never a paper cut, never gossip or betrayal or pain, to fully enter our crumbling lives. He willingly clothed himself in human flesh and blood so that he could be immersed in our joy, weep through our pain, and die in our place. God doesn't just stand on the sidelines of our lives, hoping that we'll turn to Him before lunch so that He can "nourish this food to our body." He is entirely involved with every detail of who we are, knowing our every thought (Psalm 139:2), counting every hair on our head (Luke 12:7), numbering each day we live (Job 14:5), and catching each tear we cry (Psalm 56:8). He understands our pain, sympathizes with our weakness, and has compassion for us. We see a relational God bursting through every action and every word of Scripture, boundless emotion and joy and pain pouring out of His communication with us, inviting us into the tremendous, holy adventure of knowing God personally.

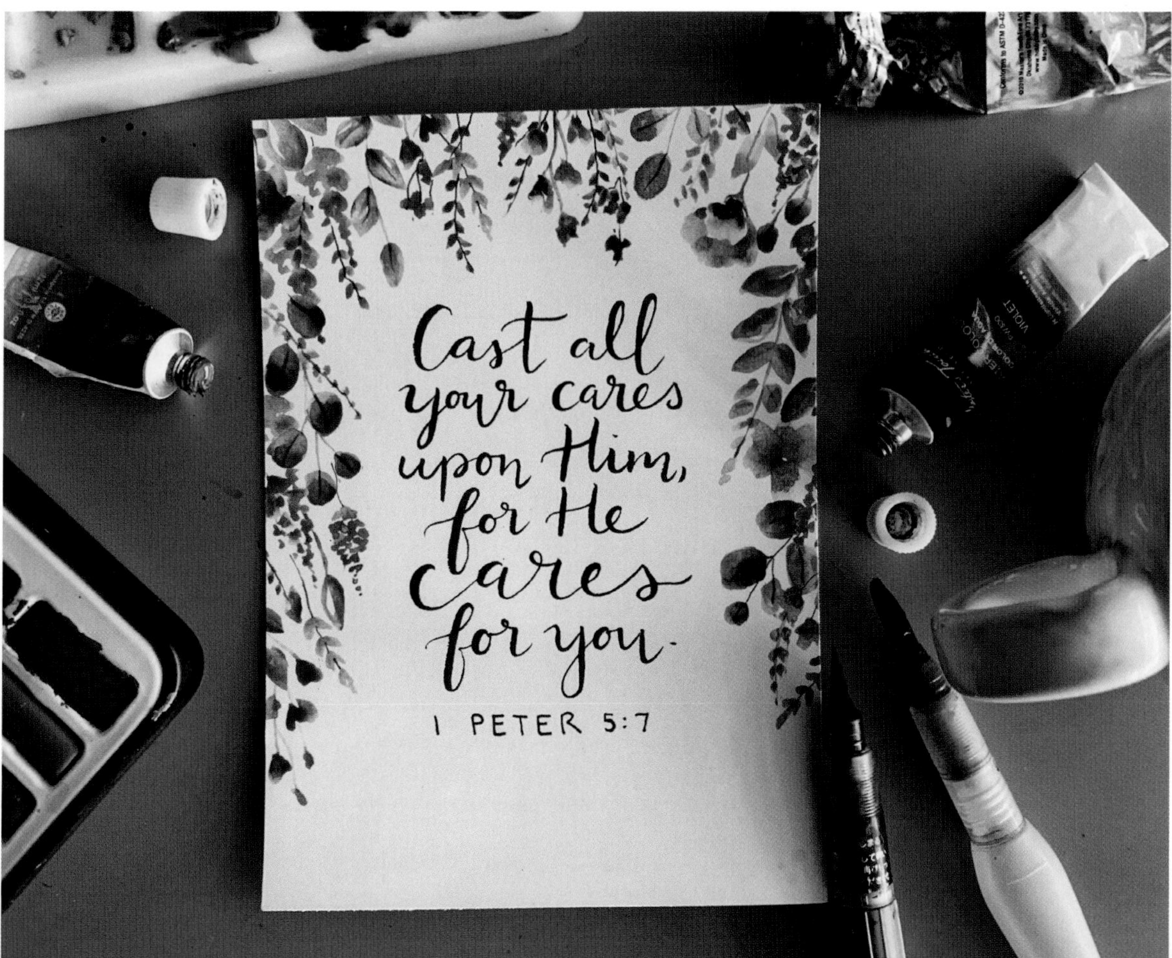

Cast all your cares upon Him, for He cares for you.
I PETER 5:7

Learning to Pray

So how do we actually get to know God better? Just like with any relationship, we spend time with Him. We pray, which means that we have a conversation with God. We talk with Him and then hear what He has to say. And how do we know what God's voice sounds like? We read His word.

Think about the person whose voice you know better than anyone else's. It might be your mom, your best friend, or your brother. My person is my husband, and I am so familiar with his voice that I can recognize it anywhere. If he were to call me at this moment from an unknown number, I'd know that it was Dan from his very first "Hey, Kristin." I would also be able to tell, from just those two words, about his general emotion—whether he was happy, irritated, in a rush, or tired. Beyond recognizing his actual, audible voice, I can also hear Dan's voice in my head as I go about my day. I have a pretty good understanding of what he would think regarding all sorts of stuff. I know if he would like a particular movie or think a certain situation was funny; I know what kinds of snacks to pick up for him at the store. I know his emotions. I know his vocabulary. How do I know all of these things? Because I've spent significant time with him.

We get to know God by spending significant time with Him, and we learn to recognize His voice by spending significant time in His word. The more we read, the more we learn about His personality. We learn how he thinks about the struggles in our world, such as poverty and refugees and loneliness. We learn His wisdom for marriages, friendships, and finances. We learn His vocabulary, His expectations of us, His pain when we reject Him, and His joy when we turn to Him. As we absorb the Bible into our lives, chapter by chapter, we learn to recognize the voice of God throughout our day because we've literally spent time with His words.

Prayer is a conversation that never ends, always ready to be picked up where it left off, weaving itself throughout every situation and task and hope and dream. Prayer journaling is a powerful opportunity to funnel some of these daily prayers into a concrete, organized space, letting us focus in on some of the specific circumstances where we're seeking the voice of God.

Pray without Ceasing

One of the benefits of journaling on thin Bible pages is that they can act as tracing paper. For this verse on prayer, I drew out the words on a separate sheet of paper and then traced over them inside my Bible, helping me achieve the exact look I wanted.

For this project, you'll need:

- Piece of scratch paper
- Ruler
- Pencil
- Eraser
- Micron 01 pen
- Brush pen
- Washi tape

1. To begin, measure in your Bible how much space you want to use, and then draw a border that size on a separate sheet of paper. My margins are 2 inches by 8 inches, but I drew my rectangle a bit wider (2.5 inches) in order to not feel too squished inside the box. I also left space at the bottom for future Bible-study application (which I discuss further in Chapter 12).

2. One way to design a verse layout is to first make a grid using different shapes, angles, and curves for your words. For this grid, I knew that I wanted the words "pray without ceasing" to be in a three-tiered banner, so I drew that first. From there, I placed two slanted boxes above the banner for "Rejoice always," and then I worked my way down below the banner for the rest of the verse, varying the width and length of my boxes in order to make it visually appealing. Once I finished, it felt like the grid was unbalanced and too heavily weighted at the bottom. I drew a curve at the very top, knowing I'd add some sort of decoration to even out the page and make it more interesting.

3. Once I was happy with my grid, I began plugging in the words of the verse. Sometimes this can take many rough drafts, and you might realize that you need to totally change your grid in order to adjust for word lengths. I chose three different fonts (cursive, all caps, and lowercase print), and I utilized them based on how I wanted to emphasize the words. For example, "rejoice" and "thanks" seem like happy words, so I drew them out as pretty, cursive words. But I wanted to emphasize the strong nature of the words "always" and "everything," so I placed them in all caps. Filler words, like "for this is the" and "in," aren't as attention grabbing, so I put them in lowercase print. In general, I recommend using a maximum of three different fonts and then repeating them through your verse. If you choose too many fonts, the piece might feel confusing and disconnected.

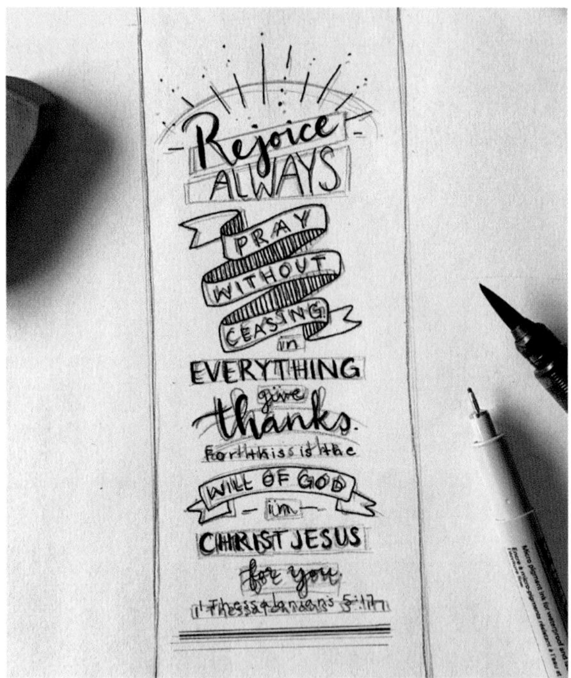

4. Once you feel happy with the grid layout and font choices, it's time to trace over all of your pencil marks with your pen. As you can see from my example, I don't necessarily follow the pencil marks exactly. As I'm drawing over the initial pencil marks, I can tell where something should be a little higher, wider, or longer. It might feel like you have blurry vision and are seeing double once you're done with your pen, but when you erase your pencil marks, your picture will become clear again.

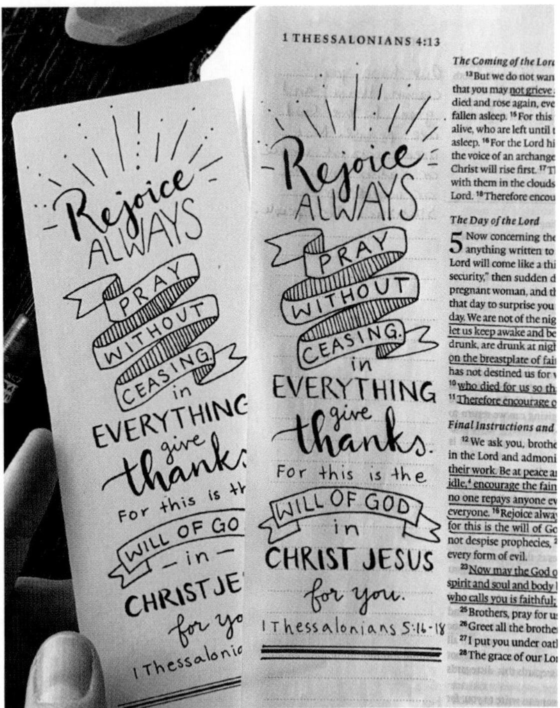

5. After erasing your pencil marks, cut out your verse and place it underneath the page in your Bible. I recommend using two pieces of washi tape (one at the top and one at the bottom) so that your piece doesn't move around as you trace it. I used a Micron 01 pen for the banners and thin words, and I used a very light hand with my brush pen for the words "rejoice," "everything," "thanks," and "Christ Jesus." Once everything was traced and dry, I gently peeled the washi tape off the original piece.

What Do We Pray About?

What should we pray about when we sit down with our prayer journals? Anything and everything! We can pray for a sibling who is going through a tough time. We can pray for God's blessing on our schoolwork. We can pray for His help in knowing if we should date a specific person. If we're lonely, we can ask God for a friend. If we're facing a deep insecurity, we can ask God for His truth. If we just got into the college of our dreams or had an amazing conversation or experienced the most perfect sunset of our lives, we can fill pages and pages with gratitude.

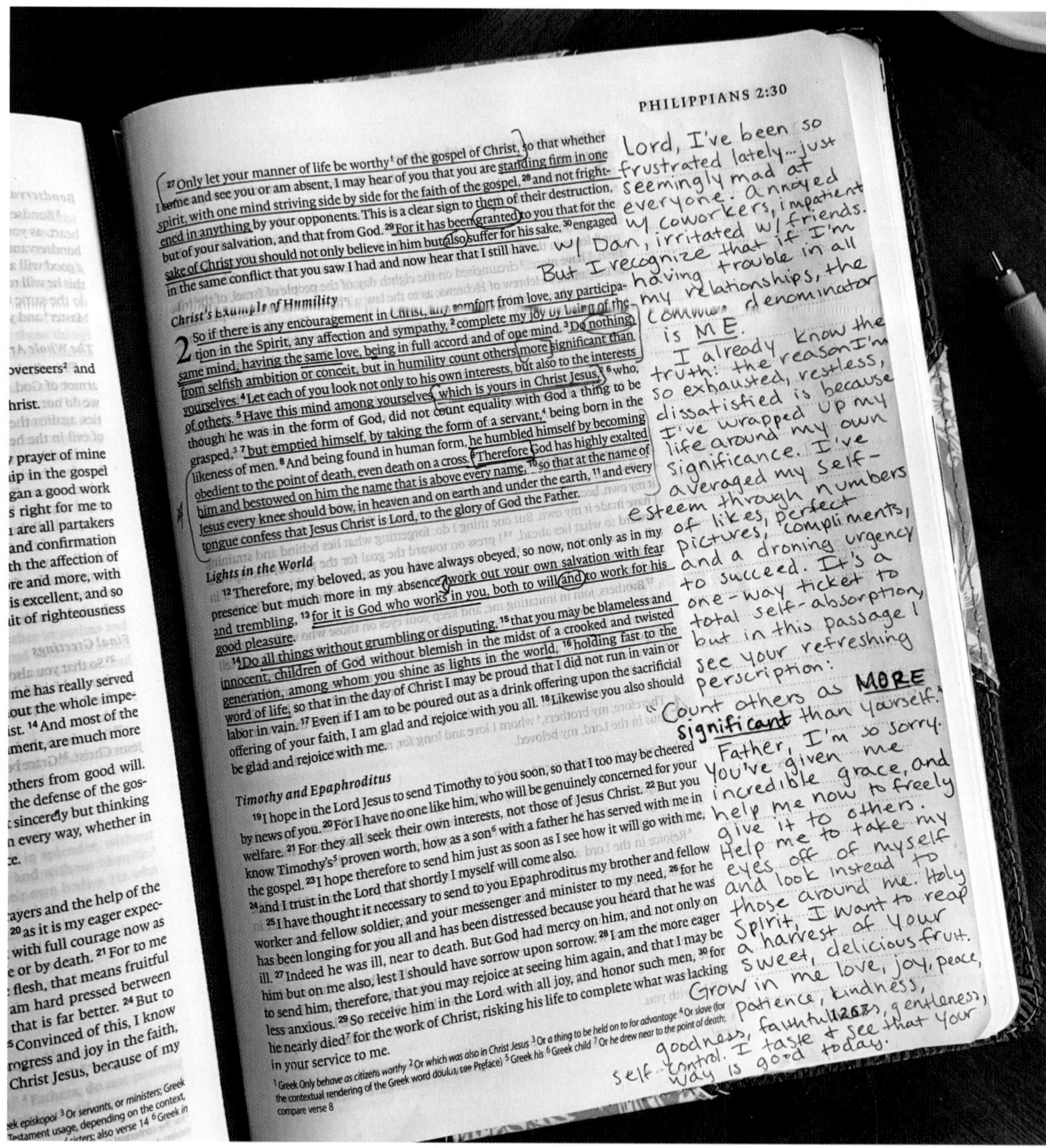

27 Only let your manner of life be worthy[1] of the gospel of Christ, so that whether I come and see you or am absent, I may hear of you that you are standing firm in one spirit, with one mind striving side by side for the faith of the gospel, 28 and not frightened in anything by your opponents. This is a clear sign to them of their destruction, but of your salvation, and that from God. 29 For it has been granted to you that for the sake of Christ you should not only believe in him but also suffer for his sake, 30 engaged in the same conflict that you saw I had and now hear that I still have.

Christ's Example of Humility

2 So if there is any encouragement in Christ, any comfort from love, any participation in the Spirit, any affection and sympathy, 2 complete my joy by being of the same mind, having the same love, being in full accord and of one mind. 3 Do nothing from selfish ambition or conceit, but in humility count others more significant than yourselves. 4 Let each of you look not only to his own interests, but also to the interests of others. 5 Have this mind among yourselves, which is yours in Christ Jesus, 6 who, though he was in the form of God, did not count equality with God a thing to be grasped,[7] 7 but emptied himself, by taking the form of a servant,[8] being born in the likeness of men. 8 And being found in human form, he humbled himself by becoming obedient to the point of death, even death on a cross. 9 Therefore God has highly exalted him and bestowed on him the name that is above every name, 10 so that at the name of Jesus every knee should bow, in heaven and on earth and under the earth, 11 and every tongue confess that Jesus Christ is Lord, to the glory of God the Father.

Lights in the World

12 Therefore, my beloved, as you have always obeyed, so now, not only as in my presence but much more in my absence, work out your own salvation with fear and trembling, 13 for it is God who works in you, both to will and to work for his good pleasure. 14 Do all things without grumbling or disputing, 15 that you may be blameless and innocent, children of God without blemish in the midst of a crooked and twisted generation, among whom you shine as lights in the world, 16 holding fast to the word of life, so that in the day of Christ I may be proud that I did not run in vain or labor in vain. 17 Even if I am to be poured out as a drink offering upon the sacrificial offering of your faith, I am glad and rejoice with you all. 18 Likewise you also should be glad and rejoice with me.

Timothy and Epaphroditus

19 I hope in the Lord Jesus to send Timothy to you soon, so that I too may be cheered by news of you. 20 For I have no one like him, who will be genuinely concerned for your welfare. 21 For they all seek their own interests, not those of Jesus Christ. 22 But you know Timothy's[5] proven worth, how as a son[6] with a father he has served with me in the gospel. 23 I hope therefore to send him just as soon as I see how it will go with me, 24 and I trust in the Lord that shortly I myself will come also. 25 I have thought it necessary to send to you Epaphroditus my brother and fellow worker and fellow soldier, and your messenger and minister to my need, 26 for he has been longing for you all and has been distressed because you heard that he was ill. 27 Indeed he was ill, near to death. But God had mercy on him, and not only on him but on me also, lest I should have sorrow upon sorrow. 28 I am the more eager to send him, therefore, that you may rejoice at seeing him again, and that I may be less anxious. 29 So receive him in the Lord with all joy, and honor such men, 30 for he nearly died[7] for the work of Christ, risking his life to complete what was lacking in your service to me.

[1] Greek Only behave as citizens worthy [2] Or which was also in Christ Jesus [3] Or a thing to be held on to for advantage [4] Or slave (for the contextual rendering of the Greek word doulos, see Preface) [5] Greek his [6] Greek child [7] Or he drew near to the point of death; compare verse 8

Handwritten prayer notes in margins:

Lord, I've been so frustrated lately... just seemingly mad at everyone, annoyed w/ coworkers, impatient w/ friends. Irritated w/ Dan. But I recognize that if I'm having trouble in all my relationships, the common denominator is ME.

I already know the truth: the reason I'm so exhausted, restless, dissatisfied is because I've wrapped up my own life around my own significance. I've averaged my self-esteem through numbers of likes, perfect pictures, compliments, and a droning urgency to succeed. It's a one-way ticket to total self-absorption, but in this passage I see your refreshing perscription:

Count others as MORE significant than yourself.

Father, I'm so sorry. You've given me incredible grace, and help me now to freely give it to others. Help me to take my eyes off of myself and look instead to those around me. Holy Spirit, I want to reap a harvest of your sweet, delicious fruit. Grow in me love, joy, peace, patience, kindness, goodness, faithfulness, gentleness, self-control. I taste + see that your way is good today.

As you can tell, I personally don't get very artistic when writing prayers in my Bible. While I do know a few people who are able to write prayers that are both gorgeously crafted and authentic, mine usually come gushing out. I've learned that if I focus too much on pretty handwriting, illustrations, or colorful additions, it ends up clouding the true purpose for why I've come: to meet with God by telling Him what's going on in my life. Don't feel upset if your prayers look messy!

Sometimes I'll open my journal with a specific situation in mind, but I'll instead feel an urge to pray for something else—maybe a friend who's going through a difficult time, an upcoming event, or just a gut-check that I should come to God with a different attitude. For example, I can't tell you how many times I've opened up my prayer journal to complain about a situation, only to feel the strong conviction of the Holy Spirit that I should instead "enter into His presence with thanksgiving" (Psalm 95:2). By the time I'm done with a thorough deep-dive into the overflowing blessings God has given me, the situation I've come to complain about seems irrelevant, totally overshadowed by the goodness of God.

I also use my prayer journal to pray about the boring, everyday stuff. At first I struggled with praying through the mundane parts of my life because it felt strange to tell God something He already knows. Why would I tell Him about my day when He saw every single thing? Why would I write out meaningful conversations if He heard every word? But then I realized something: the people who are the easiest to talk to in my life are the ones who already know the most about me. I can talk to my parents and siblings all day long, telling them for the millionth time about my favorite book or food or what I'm working on in my art business. They've already heard these things, but we talk about them over and over because we're close. My husband and I will laugh about the same story for years after it happened because we were both there and we love to relive a funny situation. We go into detail about our day, even if it was generally the same as yesterday, and we talk nonstop about our love for our son every night after we put him to bed.

The easiest people to talk to aren't the strangers who are clueless about our lives and need us to fill space with words; the easiest people to talk to are the ones who know us best and are fully present in what we have to tell them. The fact that God knows everything shouldn't stop us from talking to Him, but rather, it should increase how comfortable we feel in laying out every detail in our prayers.

PRAYER JOURNALING TIP

My one exception to telling God every detail in written form is that I normally don't rehash an argument in my journals. Have you ever gotten over an ugly fight with someone, forgiven them and moved on, only to hear about it later and get all riled up again? I frequently go back and read old journal entries, and because my prayer journal is meant to honor God and grow my spirit, I'm very intentional about not writing something down that would create anger inside me at a later date. I want to protect the forgiveness that has already been worked out in my heart.

The way I do this is by writing down a vague description of what happened ("God, I'm so sad about the fight I had with my friend"), but not the exact thing we argued about. If I need to really work through the details, I'll do that in my head, writing down my prayers as God reveals the ways in which I was wrong and contributed to the problem. After wrestling with the issue and coming to a conclusion with God's help, I'll also thank God at the end for His mercy in teaching me how to have peace in my relationships. This way, I know that if I read the prayer in the future, the emotion it will stir in my heart is gratitude for reconciliation and a reminder of the ways God has helped me grow.

Prayer Points Page

When we're building a habit of prayer in our lives, it can be helpful to have "prayer points," or specific things we remind ourselves to pray about on a daily basis. This way, our hearts and minds are creating a pattern for prayer that includes more than just praying for personal, immediate problems. Using prayer points can turn our eyes beyond ourselves and remind us to lift up our family, friends, city, and world to Christ. For this Prayer Points Page, I used one of the thicker, blank pages at the very beginning of my Bible. This let me add more watercolor than a normal Bible page can handle, and it also makes it easy to find every morning when I pray.

For this project, you'll need:

- Ruler
- Pencil
- Eraser
- Piece of cardstock, cut into a small rectangle
- Piece of protective cardboard to layer underneath page
- Two colors of watercolor paint (I used purple and turquoise)
- Round paintbrush
- Micron 05, 03, and 01 pens

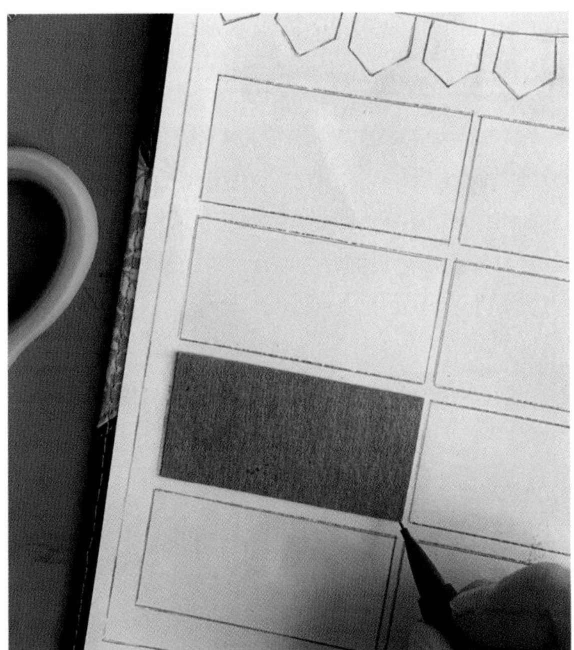

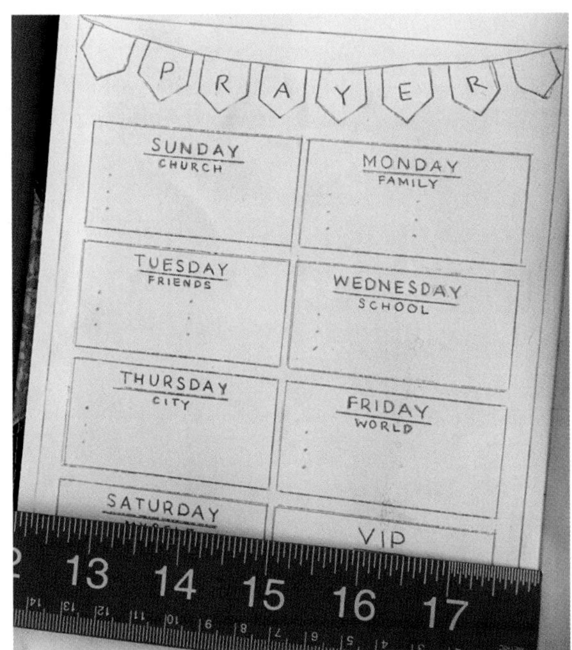

1. As with the Scripture Memory Page project in Chapter 7, begin by using your ruler and pencil to make a border around your page. Then, starting from the top left corner and swooping to the top right corner, draw a simple banner with eight flags. To make uniform rectangles for your prayer points, cut out a small rectangle from a piece of cardstock and trace it eight times (four in each column).

2. Use your banner to make a header for your page by writing "prayer" inside the flags. You will have one extra flag on each side. Inside your boxes, write each day of the week in all caps, and then that day's prayer point underneath a straight line. You can choose any prayer points you'd like and place them in any order you'd like. My choices were church, family, friends, school, city, world, and myself. In my final box, I wrote VIP (Very Important Prayers), which are specific items I'd like to pray for every day, regardless of that day of the week's particular prayer topic.

3. To paint the outside of the boxes in an ombré style, use the technique described under Blending Colors on page 37. (Before you begin, remember to layer a piece of protective cardboard underneath your page.) Fully soak your round brush in water, then saturate it in a deep purple (I'm using Smart Watercolor's C33). Begin painting at the top left corner of your border, carefully working around the pencil marks you've created. As you move right and down, gradually lighten the purple by adding water and using less paint.

4. When you get about halfway through, clean your brush and saturate it in turquoise (I'm using Smart Watercolor's C30). Work from the bottom left corner to meet your purple watercolor in the middle, gradually lightening your turquoise by using more water and less paint.

5. After the paint at the top of the page is completely dry, paint the inside of the flags the same color as the bottom, making sure that the color is transparent enough to show the prayer header.

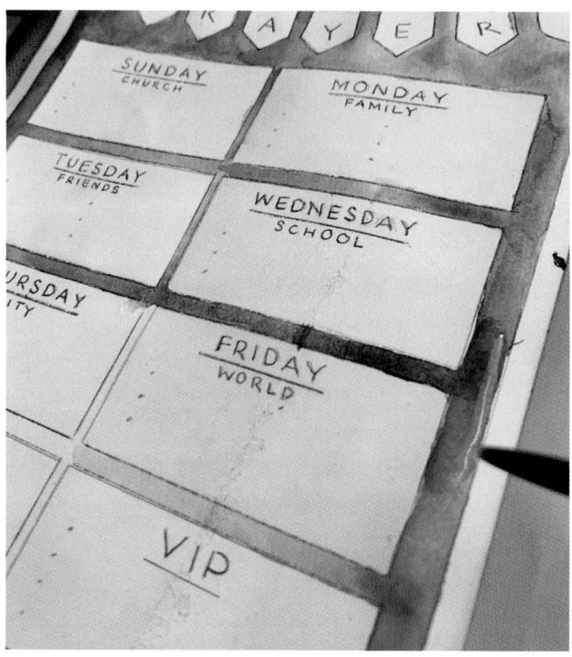

6. When your two colors meet in the middle, they might need extra help blending together. In this instance, I used the paint-lifting technique described on page 38. To do this, clean your brush and dip it in clear water, letting the bristles soak up as much water as they can. Take your fully wet brush to the page and "paint" the area you'd like to blend, allowing the water to form a controlled puddle on your page. Next, dry your brush off on a paper towel, and then go back to the puddle with the brush to soak up the water you've just painted. Continue drying off your brush and then soaking up the water until the area you're working with has "lifted" its saturated color and appears more blended.

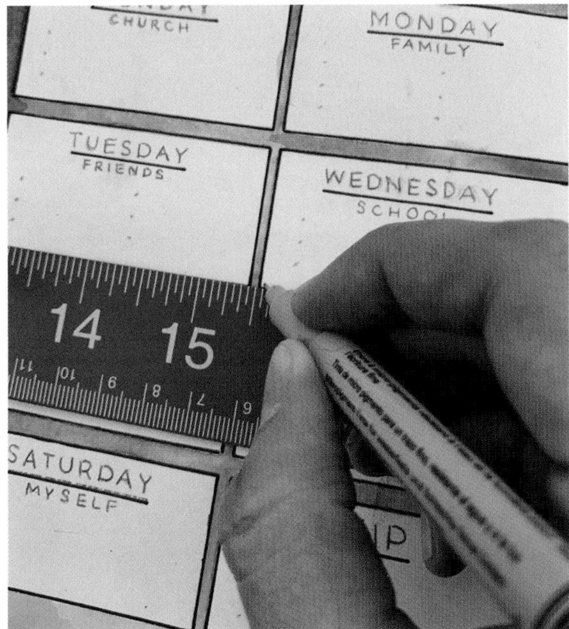

7. After your watercolor has fully dried, it's time to go over your pencil marks with your Micron pen, using a ruler to ensure straight lines. For the outside border, rectangles, flag, and prayer header, use a thick Micron pen, like the 08 or 05, to create a bold contrast. For the header words inside the rectangles, use a slightly thinner Micron pen, like the 05 or 03.

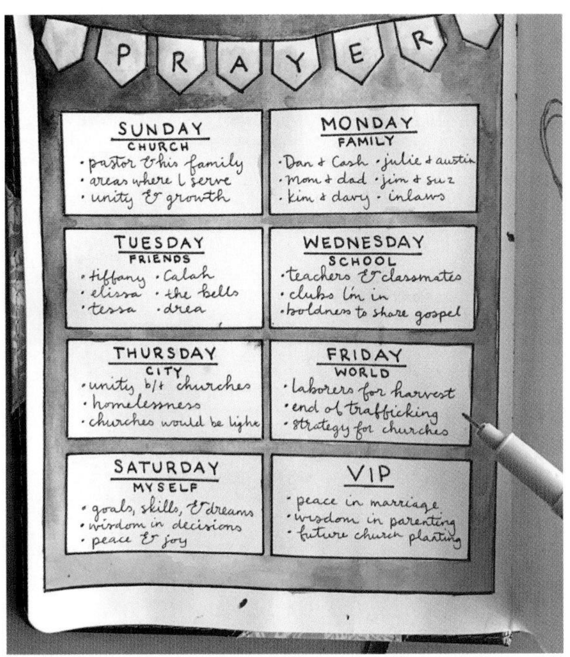

8. It's time to add in your prayer points! Under each header, use your Micron 01 pen to write in a few things you'd like to pray for every week. You can make this broad (e.g., under "family," you could write "parents, siblings," e.g.), or you can make it specific. I chose to write out actual names because it helps me to be more missional in my thinking, prompting individual prayer requests for others rather than general prayers. I recommend using cursive writing or a different font than your headers in order to make a clear distinction between them.

I've noticed a powerful interaction between art, praying for others, and memorizing the Bible: I always want to draw verses I love to give to people I'm praying for! As you read through your Bible and pray for people on your list, you'll come across verses that will be an encouragement to them. Examples are comforting verses like Isaiah 43:2 for someone going through a difficult time, event-related verses like Psalm 139 for a birthday or 1 Corinthians 13 for a wedding, and inspiring verses like Ecclesiastes 9:10 for someone starting a new job or entering into a new phase of their life. The possibilities are endless! The simple act of drawing out a verse, pairing it with an encouraging note, and popping it in the mail will speak volumes about your love and care for the people God has placed in your life.

What Part of the Bible Should I Use for Prayer Journaling?

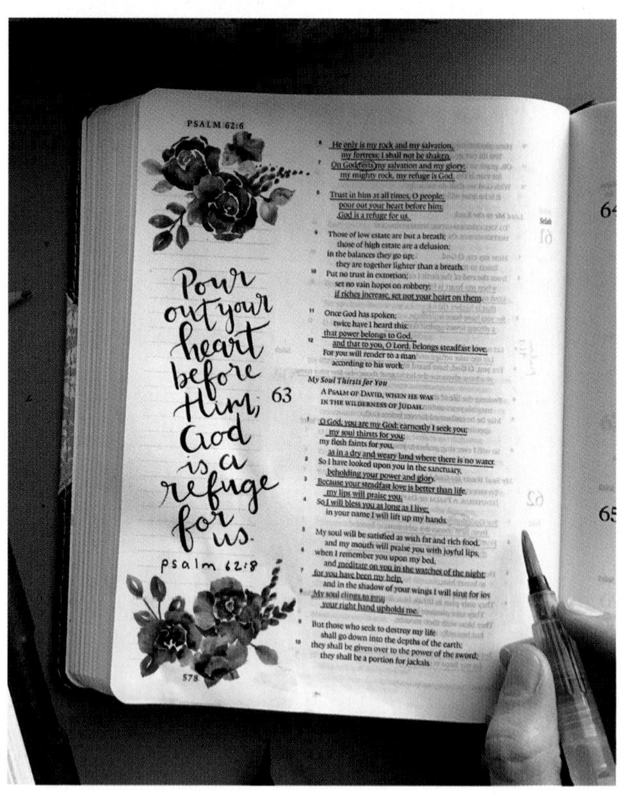

My favorite place to write out prayers in my journaling Bible is the book of Psalms, because it's an entire book of written prayers, in both poetry and song form. Many of the Psalms were written by David during some unbelievably stressful times of his life: defeating a giant, living as a fugitive, avoiding assassination, being crowned king, fighting wars, repenting for murdering an innocent officer and committing adultery . . . this man faced some severe challenges! Through observing David's internal processing of his circumstances, we have a powerful example of what it means to bring the full, raw experiences of our lives before God, not holding back our questions, doubts, or sadness. Many Psalms include both thanksgiving and anguish, such as awe toward God's power and dismay at His silence. They provide us with a blueprint for expressing honesty and vulnerability before God, bringing Him our full heart while still holding foremost to His goodness and plan.

Chapter Nine

HYMNS AND SONG LYRICS

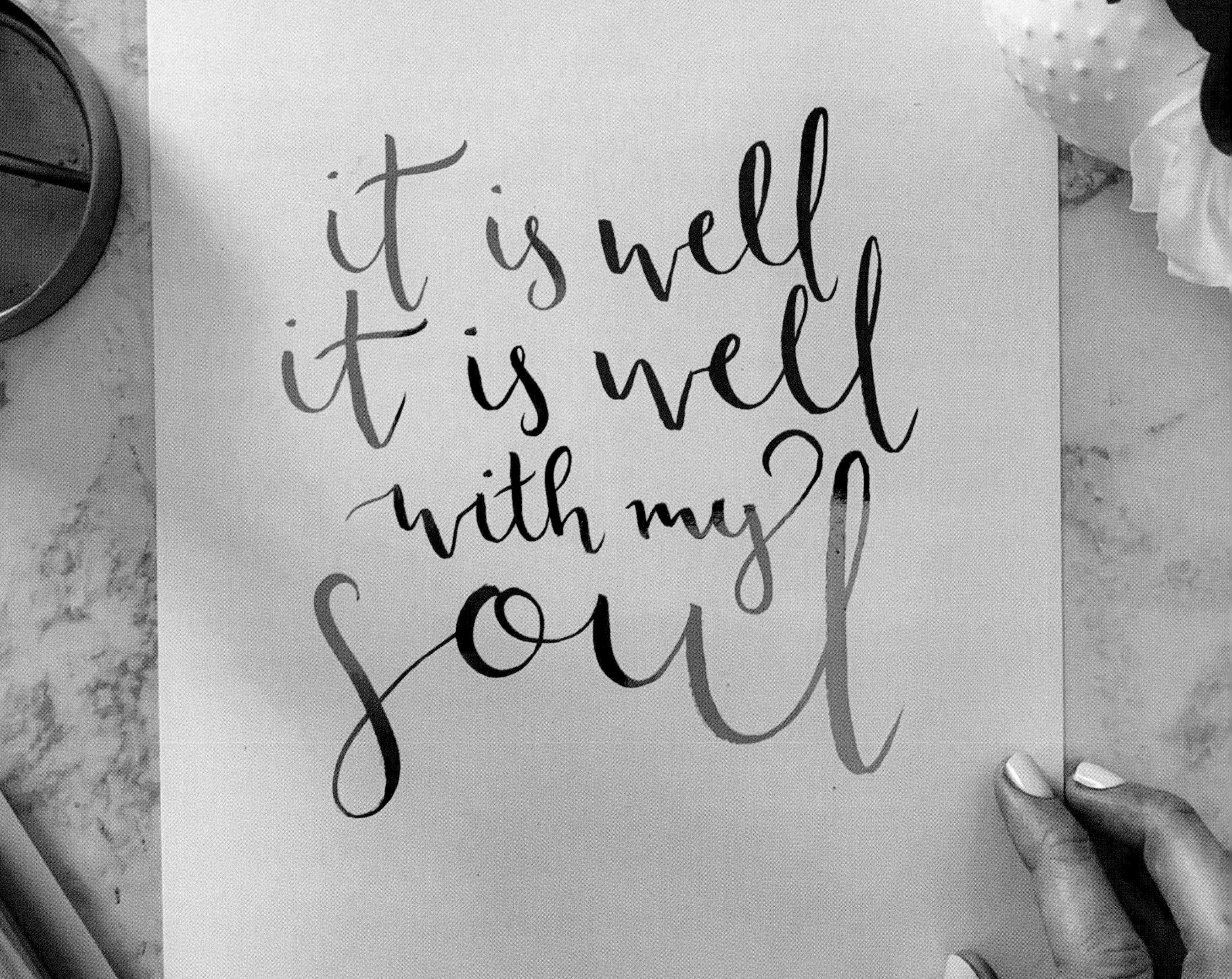

Have you ever read your Bible and come across a verse that you recognize from a song? When this happens to me, the melody immediately pops into my head, and I realize that I had the verse I'm reading memorized all along! Scripture set to music has been an incredibly effective way of helping Jews and Christians internalize the Word of God throughout history. In fact, we even have evidence of Jesus singing a hymn with His disciples (which would have been a Psalm from the Old Testament) on the night he was arrested. From Genesis to Revelation, the Bible shows us the profound role of music in our faith.

In Genesis 2, we see Adam burst into song at the first sight of Eve. In Exodus 15, the Israelites sing at the Red Sea after God delivers them from the Egyptians. In Joshua 6, the people blow trumpets and lift up shouts of praise as the walls of Jericho fall before them. In 2 Chronicles 20, an entire battle is won solely through worshipping God. The word "Psalms" actually means sacred songs, and in Zephaniah 3, we learn that God Himself "rejoices over us with singing."

In the New Testament, we continue to find music woven into the culture of Christians. In Acts 16, Paul and Silas are singing a hymn when an angel frees them from prison. The books of Colossians and Ephesians both instruct us to sing with other believers when we get together. Finally, in Revelation, we see songs lifted up before the throne of God in heaven, declaring God's redemption of "every tribe and tongue and people and nation" (7:9).

The more we read the Bible, the more we can delight when we discover that verses we've learned are written into songs we love. Some songs quote the Bible directly, some summarize passages, and some give a sweeping narrative of the whole Bible story. I'm so grateful for worship artists who study theology as much as they study music; they are literally filling the mouths of Christians worldwide with the truth of God's extravagant, redemptive character.

for the
Lord your God
is
living among you.
He is a
mighty savior.
He will take
delight in you
with gladness,
With His love
He will
Calm all your fears
He will
rejoice over you
with
joyful songs.
ZEPHANIAH 3:17

My favorite songs to write in my journaling Bible are hymns because the profound lyrics often include direct quotes from Scripture. For example, take a look at the beloved hymn "Great Is Thy Faithfulness" below. Each line comes directly from the Bible.

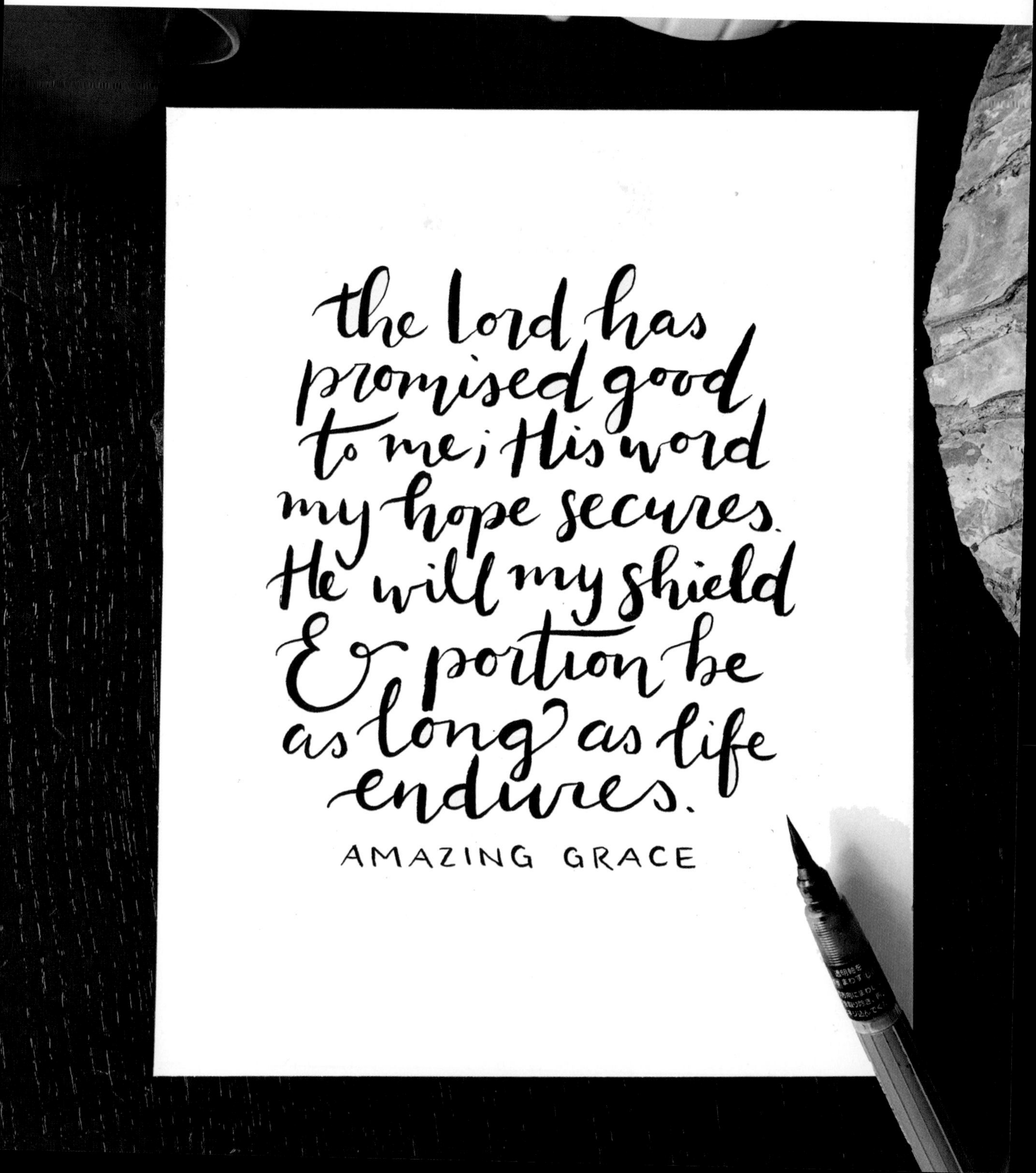

the lord has promised good to me; His word my hope secures. He will my shield & portion be as long as life endures.
AMAZING GRACE

VERSES FOR "GREAT IS THY FAITHFULNESS"

When I started looking for the Scripture verses that make up "Great Is Thy Faithfulness," I decided to call my dad for help, and he did not disappoint. My dad first gave his life to Christ at age seventeen, and when he started college, the guy in charge of his campus ministry announced he was stepping down. When nobody else volunteered to lead, my dad stepped in. He knew he needed to grow in his understanding of the Bible, and so at nineteen years old, he began reading ten chapters of the Bible every day (the equivalent of reading the entire Bible three times a year), taking detailed notes on each chapter. This went on for several years in a row, and as a result, he has significant portions of the Bible memorized. Without any prior knowledge that I was going to ask him for help, and without looking at a computer, my dad was able to tell me each of the verses below off the top of his head (#goals).

"Great Is Thy Faithfulness," by Thomas Obadiah Chisholm

Great is Thy faithfulness (Lamentations 3:23)

*O God my Father (*Matthew 6:9)

There is no shadow of turning with Thee (James 1:17)

Thou changest not (Malachi 3:6)

Thy compassions they fail not (Lamentations 3:22)

As Thou hast been, Thou forever will be (Hebrews 13:8)

Great is Thy faithfulness, Great is Thy faithfulness (Lamentations 3:23)

Morning by morning new mercies I see (Lamentations 3:23)

And all I have needed Thy hand hath provided (Philippians 4:19)

Great is Thy faithfulness, Lord unto me (Lamentations 3:23)

Summer and winter, and springtime and harvest, (Genesis 8:22)

Sun, moon and stars in their courses above (Psalm 148:3)

Join with all nature in manifold witness (Psalm 19:1–4)

To Thy great faithfulness, mercy and love. (Lamentations 3:23)

“Great Is Thy Faithfulness” Calligraphy

Since Lamentations 3:23 is one of the verses that make up the chorus of “Great Is Thy Faithfulness,” I wanted to write the lyrics down boldly in the margins of my Bible.

For this project, you’ll need:

- Protective cardstock to layer underneath your page
- Yellow watercolor paint
- Round paintbrush
- Pencil
- Eraser
- Separate sheet of paper if you’d like to trace your words
- Brush pen

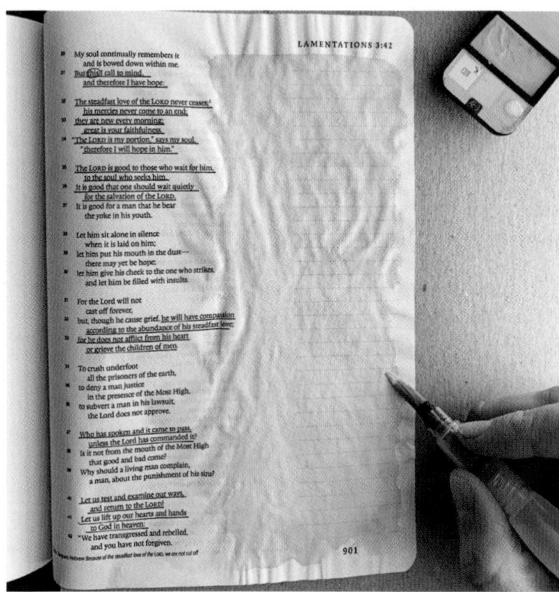

1. Before you begin, place a piece of thick cardstock behind your page in order to protect the pages underneath from getting wet. Next, dip your paintbrush in water and saturate it in bright yellow paint. (I chose this color to evoke morning sunshine because of the words “Morning by morning, new mercies I see.”) Using the wash technique described under Paint Wash on page 39, place your brush at the top right of the margin and gently wash your color toward the bottom of the page, adding more water and using less paint as you go. Once I finished with my first layer, I felt like adding some darker color to the bottom left of the wash would make it more interesting, so I wet that area again and layered it with a second coat of paint.

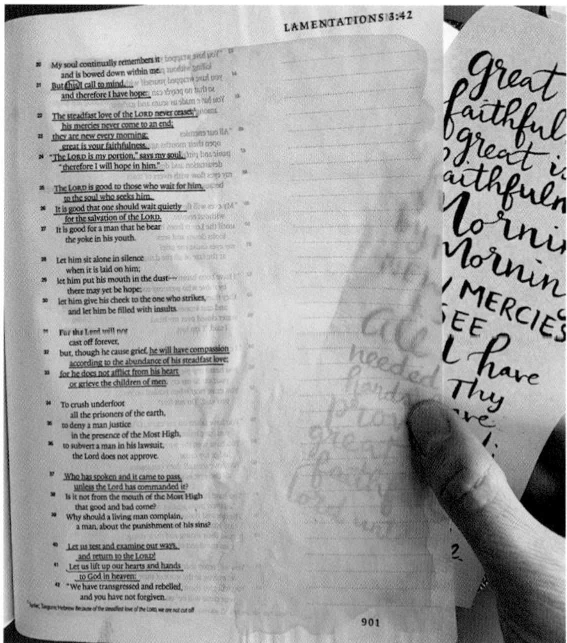

2. I decided to first design these lyrics on another sheet of paper and then trace them onto the page, the same way I did with the "Pray without Ceasing" verse in Chapter 8. I wasn't sure if my pen marks would show through the watercolor, but they weren't difficult to see at all.

I recommend using a very light touch because you will need to erase them gently in order to not change the texture of your watercolor.

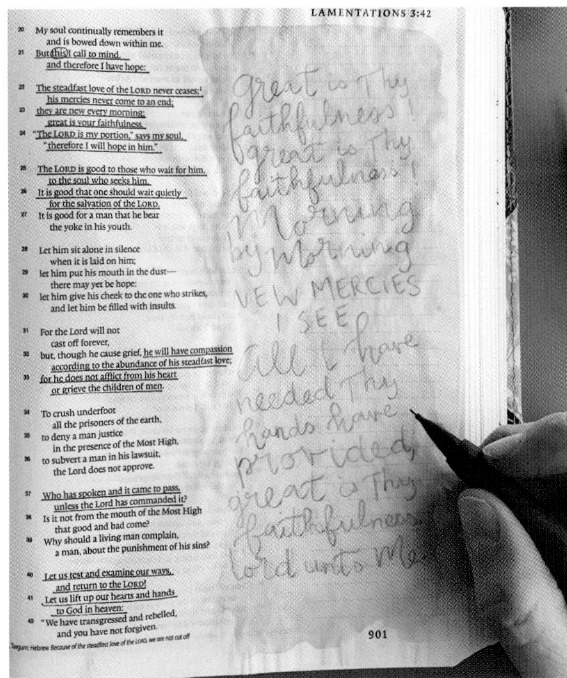

3. After your watercolor is completely dry, trace your lyrics with a soft pencil.

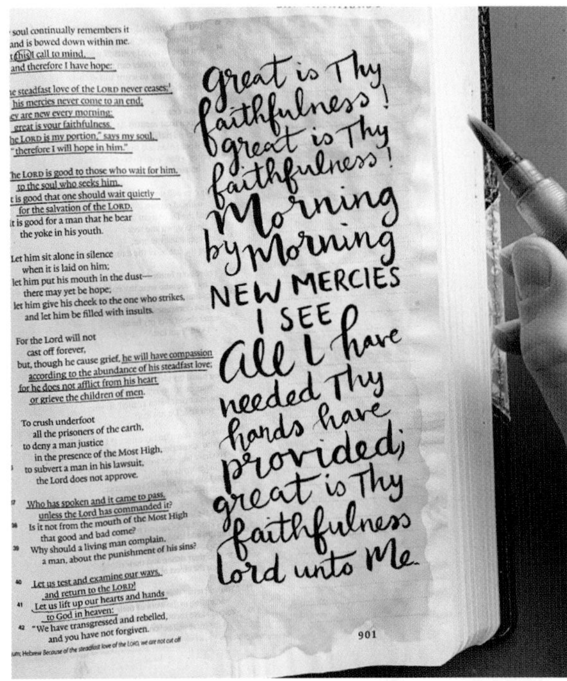

4. Go over your pencil marks with your brush pen, let the words dry, and then gently erase the pencil marks underneath.

Hymns Showcase the Story of the Bible

Another reason I love hymns is that many of them do the deep, intelligent work of digging into a specific verse and then finding examples throughout the Bible that connect to the truth of that verse. This frequently includes a full picture of humanity's sin, Jesus's death and resurrection, and our future in heaven (an example of this is a hymn you might hear on the radio or sing in your own church: "In Christ Alone"). For this reason, churches all over the world still sing hymns that were written hundreds of years ago. They aren't fad songs that burst onto the Christian scene and then exit our churches just as quickly; these songs have instead taken root in our faith's very culture, helping Christians worldwide grow in our understanding of and love for God.

Some hymns were written by people at a very young age, like the hymn "My Jesus, I Love Thee." William Featherston (1846–72) penned these lyrics when he was just sixteen years old, and he died only ten years later at the age of twenty-six. Even though he lived a short time on earth, his life produced a song that has blessed millions of people. When I read his lyrics, I'm so inspired that a teenager paired together his love for Christ and his familiarity with the Bible to make something that the church is still singing 160 years later. I imagine him now, the reality of his final stanza come to life, singing his hymn before the actual throne of Jesus.

"My Jesus, I Love Thee," by William Featherston

My Jesus, I love Thee, I know Thou art mine;
for Thee all the follies of sin I resign.

My gracious Redeemer, my Savior art Thou;
if ever I loved Thee, my Jesus, 'tis now.

I love Thee because Thou hast first loved me,
and purchased my pardon on Calvary's tree;

I love Thee for wearing the thorns on Thy brow;
if ever I loved Thee, my Jesus, 'tis now.

I'll love Thee in life, I will love Thee in death,
And praise Thee as long as Thou lendest me breath;

And say when the death dew lies cold on my brow,
If ever I loved Thee, my Jesus, 'tis now.

In mansions of glory and endless delight,
I'll ever adore Thee in heaven so bright;

I'll sing with the glittering crown on my brow;
If ever I loved Thee, my Jesus, 'tis now.

Because hymns usually have references from all over Scripture, it can be difficult to choose where in your journaling Bible to letter the lyrics. One option is to write the hymn throughout your Bible, splitting up the various stanzas next to the verses where they're found.

Another option is to choose a stanza that helps you understand the Scripture verse it's based on in a new light. For example, the hymn "How Deep the Father's Love for Us" has multiple direct Bible references, but I chose to letter the third and fourth stanzas next to John 19:30, where Jesus is on the cross and says, "It is finished." This is because this hymn helps me insert myself (my sin, my hand) into the story of Jesus's crucifixion. It stirs in me love for Jesus, humility toward others, and gratitude for His forgiveness.

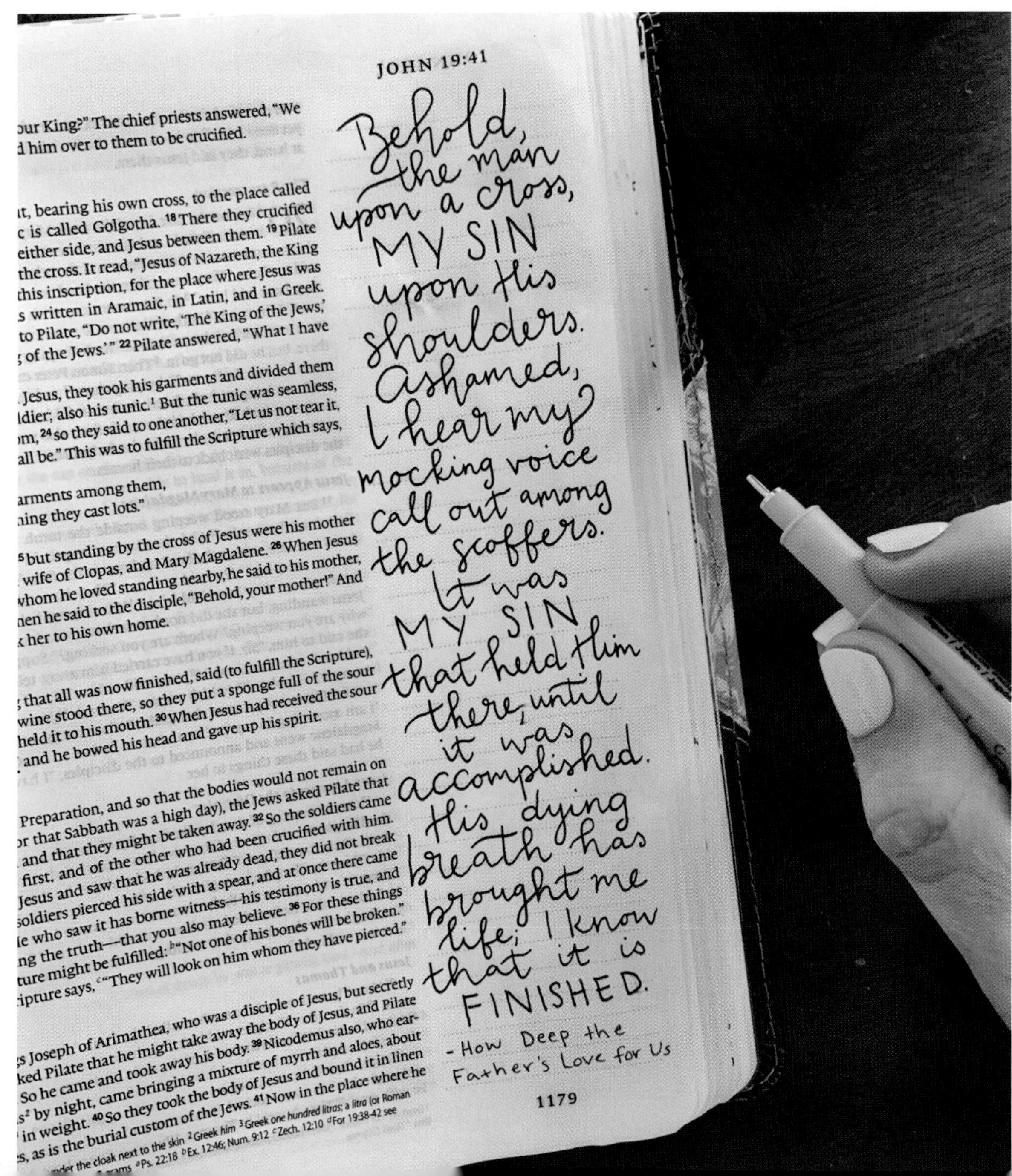

Chapter Ten

SERMON NOTES

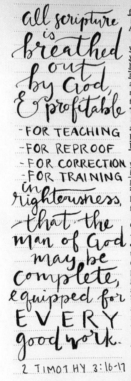

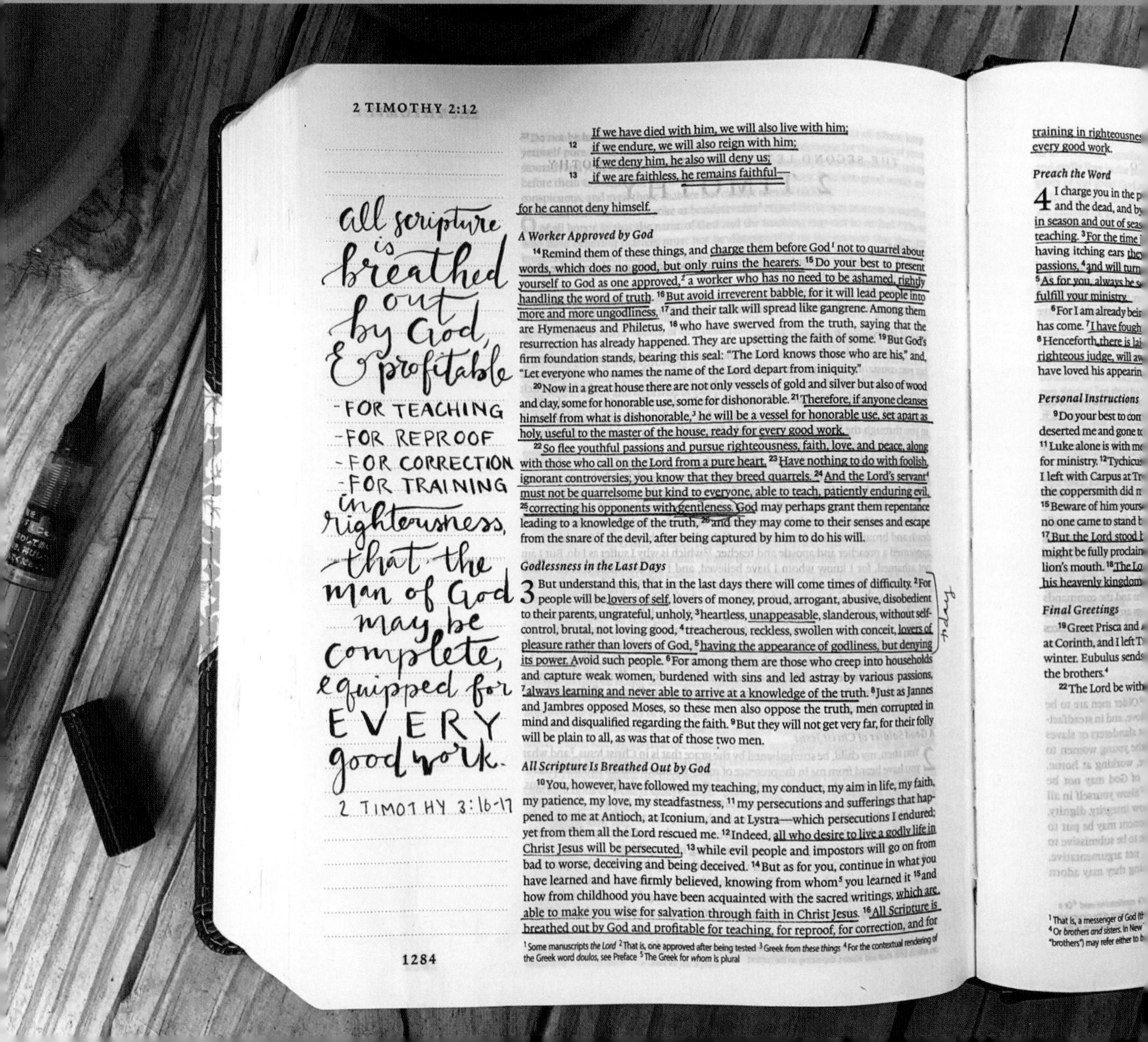

I'm super lucky to have heard a ton of amazing sermons throughout my life, in church services, youth groups, summer camps, and missionary trips. But one unfortunate consequence is the number of random pieces of paper scattered throughout my house where I've haphazardly scribbled the "ah-ha!" moments of the messages. I've never liked taking notes on my phone (I think many artists probably feel this way) because my brain seems to think better when I have a pen in my hand. As a result, I have countless scraps of paper, torn-off pieces of church bulletins, and crumpled napkins with hardly legible notes written on them. They are in boxes in my closet, stuffed between the pages of my Bible, and taped onto random pages of journals.

A few months ago, I was preparing my own message to speak to a group of college students about gratitude, and I remembered hearing a sermon from my pastor where he explained a specific verse in a helpful way. I tore apart my room looking for my notes from that sermon, and unfortunately, I never found them. At that moment, I made a decision: all of my sermon notes needed to be consolidated into one specific place, where I could easily access and review them. And what better place is there than directly next to the passage from which my pastor is preaching? My journaling Bible gives me the perfect space to organize

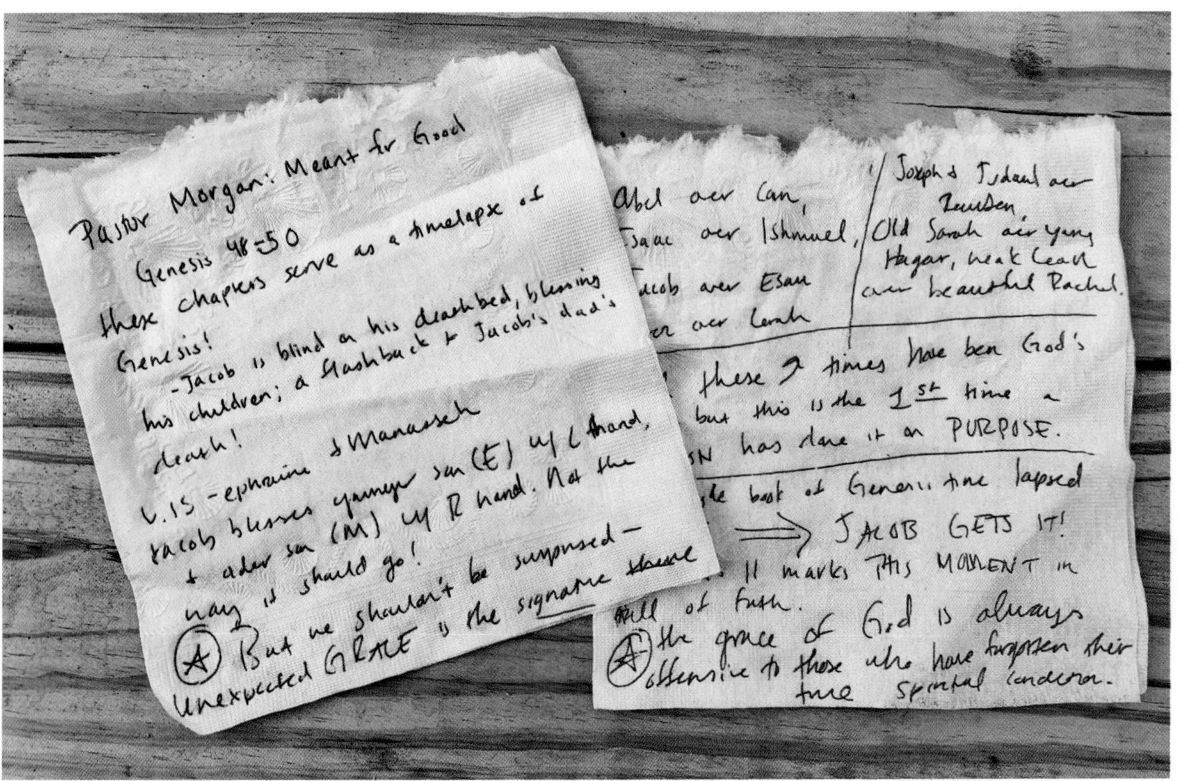

verse explanations, write down meaningful quotes from my pastor, and further study the context surrounding the verses from the sermon.

Our pastors put a ton of hard work into preparing a feast of God's word for us every week, and looking back on our notes is another way that we can feed on God's faithfulness. When we reread the same verses years later, glancing at our notes in the margins, we can remember the teaching we heard and continue to build on our understanding of the Bible.

These are my notes from a sermon given by my pastor, Morgan Stephens, at Mosaic Church Austin. Genesis has been my favorite book of the Bible for a long time, and he explained a scene from the book in a way I'd never before considered. For this reason, I decided to combine general writing with a few illustrations, helping me to better remember and understand the message.

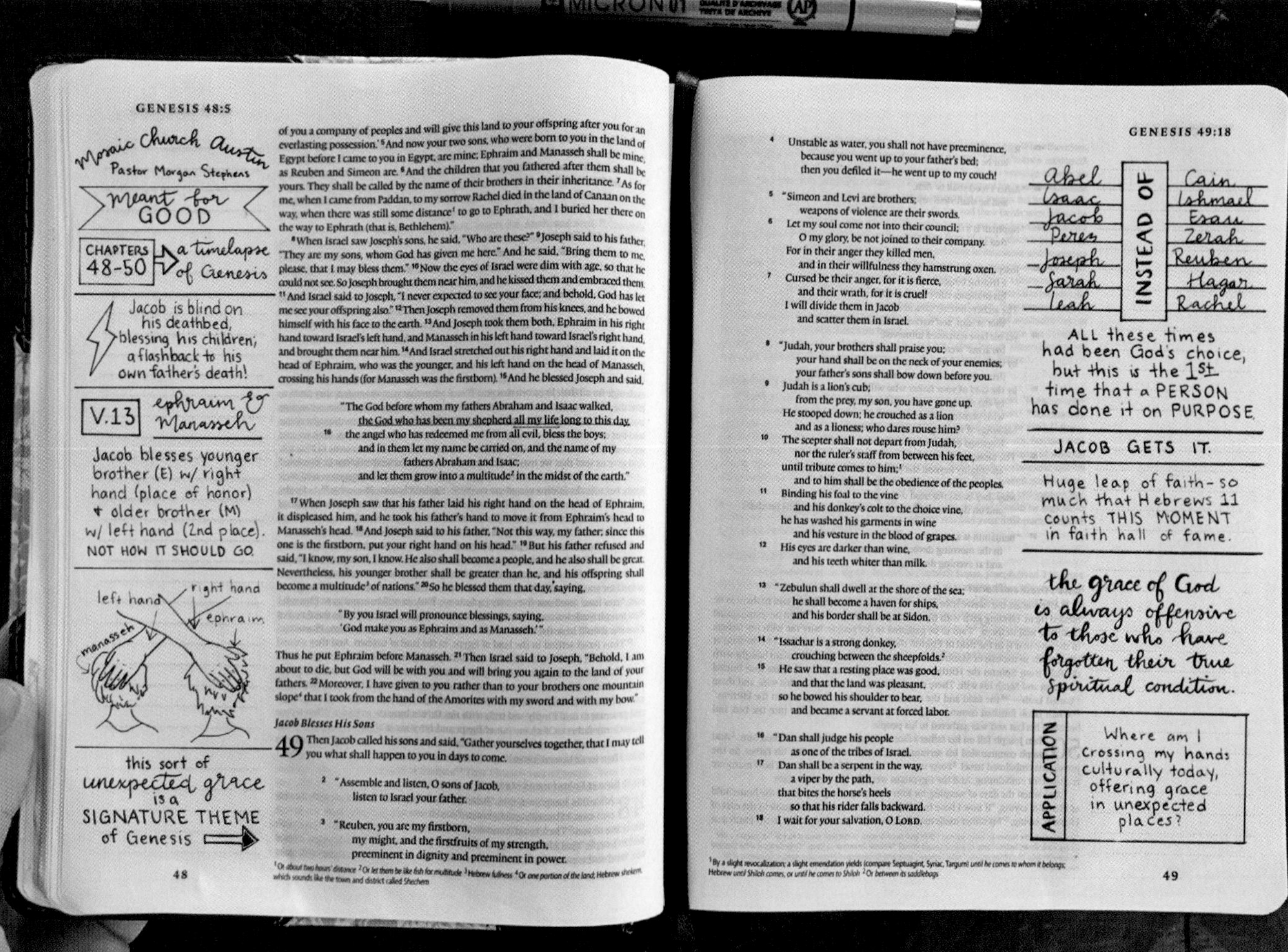

Practical Strategies for Note Taking

As with all of the strategies above, it's important to remember that the goal of taking sermon notes in our journaling Bibles is to learn, celebrate, and grow in our understanding of God's word. The focus is the message; notes are just an aid.

ANALYZE YOUR NOTE-TAKING PERSONALITY. If you are able to focus completely on the message while jotting down notes inside your Bible, then go for it! But if you, like me, get distracted by trying to arrange everything perfectly, take notes on a separate sheet of paper and then transfer them to your Bible when you get home.

DON'T TRY TO WRITE DOWN EVERY WORD OF THE SERMON. It's impossible to write as fast as your pastor talks, so remind yourself to focus on what he's saying, and then summarize the main highlights from his message. This will help you to see the full picture of the sermon rather than getting bogged down in individual sentences.

PICK A SINGLE PAGE TO WRITE ALL OF YOUR NOTES OR SPREAD OUT THE SERMON NOTES NEXT TO THE DIFFERENT VERSES FROM THE SERMON. Sometimes our pastors preach out of a single chapter of the Bible for the entire sermon, and sometimes they use many verses from all throughout Scripture to deep-dive into a specific topic. This can make it a little bit more difficult to decide where to insert our sermon notes. In this case, choose what makes the most sense based on the message and the way you personally like to organize your thoughts.

Chapter Eleven

SCRIPTURE ILLUSTRATIONS

One of my biggest fears about becoming a mom was knowing I'd be sleep deprived with a newborn. Much to my delight, my son, Cassius, slept beautifully for the first three months. But at month four, he began waking up multiple times throughout the night as well as at 5:00 a.m. on the dot, every single day. For the first few weeks, hearing his wee-hour cries sent despair through my body, and I got out of bed exhausted and hopeless. But one day, I decided to take him on a walk. I loaded him in his stroller, and we trudged our way past the neighborhood houses, then turned a corner to an open field. I literally gasped for air at the sight in front of me: orange stripes shooting across the sky, navy-blue clouds laced with striking golden edges, a soft pink glow cast over every tree and blade of grass. The sunrise was glorious.

From that day on, my early-morning despair was replaced with early-morning anticipation. I'd get Cassius out of bed, shuffle out the front door, and head to the field. The first few days I walked slowly, but I soon found myself chasing the sunrise, telling Cassius, "Let's hurry, it's almost here!" Sometimes I stood in silent awe, and sometimes I literally shouted into the open field, "Lord, this is GORGEOUS!" The sunrise was changing my life because it was changing my day. It started my morning with hope, aligning my heart to God's beauty and invoking celebration.

In the beginning, God
created the heavens & the earth.
GENESIS 1:1

I also found myself analyzing the creativity in front of me, wanting to peg the specific red hues and trying to understand the shading, shapes, and color combinations. After getting back home, I'd rush to my little studio with an urgency to mix creamy yellows and bold oranges on my paint palette. Every morning, I was struck by the majesty of God's creativity, and every morning it produced creative worship inside of me.

Our Creative God

God is a creative God. In fact, this is the first thing He chooses to tell us about Himself in the very first sentence of the Bible. In his book *Called to Create*, author Jordan Raynor says, "Before we learn that God is loving, holy, or merciful, we learn that He is creative." From cacti to waterfalls to Jupiter to hippos, we see wild variation, detail, and color in all He has made. He is an artist, and we are made in His image. We are created to create.

> Before the Bible tells us that God is loving, holy, or merciful, we learn that He is creative.
>
> JORDAN RAYNOR
> CALLED TO CREATE

Evidence of God's creative nature is written throughout the Bible. After the opening act of creation in Genesis, His artistry unfolds in architecture and interior design, as He gives precise instructions about colors, fabrics, materials, and measurements for the Tabernacle (a portable temple for the Jews as they traveled to the Promised Land). And then, in Exodus 31, something beautiful happens. For the first time in Scripture, we see that someone is filled with the Spirit of God, and surprisingly, it isn't Moses, Joshua, or a tribe leader. It's an *artist*. God's Spirit fills Bezalel "with ability and intelligence, with knowledge and all craftsmanship, to devise artistic designs . . ." (Exodus 31:3–4). Friend, if you've ever doubted whether God cares about art, let it be put to rest.

In Isaiah, we see God as a potter. In Zephaniah, we see God as a singer. In the New Testament, we find out that Jesus was a carpenter. Through the parables, we discover Him as a powerful storyteller. And over and over, we find that God is the ultimate Maker, making all things new (Revelation 21:5), making everything beautiful in its time (Ecclesiastes 3:11), making all things work together for the good of those who love Him (Romans 8:28).

As Christian artists, sometimes it feels like our work isn't important. Other times, it feels like it only matters if it's profound and full of brilliant truths, written with an emotional caption on social media and able to connect with others. But the truth is that the simple act of creating something as unto the Lord is worship. It's bearing His image in a tangible, unique way. When you illustrate images in your Bible as an expression of your love for God, you are imitating the Creator.

Ideas for Illustration

The Bible is rich with images for us to illustrate. Below are some specific themes, each with a few examples.

Nature

- Creation (all throughout the Bible!)
- Mountains (Mount Sinai, Calvary, faith to move a mountain, mountains thrown into the sea)
- Water (the flood, still waters, living water, Jesus calming the storm, baptism)
- Trees (the man who trusts in the Lord is like a tree, the tree of life, vine and the branches)
- Gardening (Garden of Eden, Garden of Gethsemane, sowing and reaping, the plentiful harvest, seeds on various soil)
- Fruit (fruit of the Spirit, bearing much fruit)
- Flowers (lilies of the field)

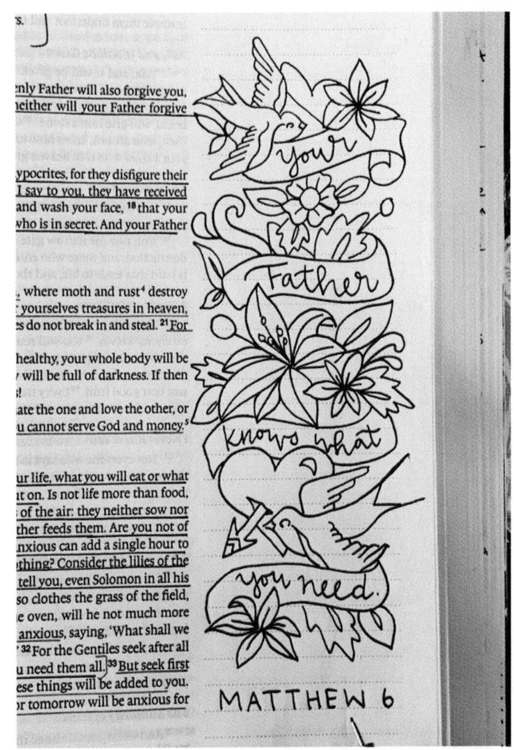

Animals

- Lions (Lion of Judah, lion and the lamb, Daniel in the lion's den)
- Sheep (the Lord is my shepherd, leaving the ninety-nine in search of the one)
- Birds (hiding under His wings, soaring like eagles, more valuable than sparrows)
- Insects (hardworking ants, locusts, plagues)

- Donkeys (Balaam, Mary on the donkey, Jesus riding in on a donkey)
- Fish (fishers of men, coin in fish's mouth, Jonah)

The Body

- Heart (let not your heart be troubled, love the Lord with all your heart, new heart in you)
- Body (body of Christ, body is a temple of the Holy Spirit, one body / one church)
- Eyes (eyes of the Lord throughout the earth, open the eyes of our heart, healing verses)
- Hands (His righteous right hand, establish the work of our hands, engraved on His hands)

Jewels

- Foundations laid with gems, streets of gold / pearly gates, pearl of great price, wisdom more precious than jewels

Battle

- Arrows, armor, towers for battle, chariots, warriors

Clothing

- Crowns (crown of life, casting our crowns before the throne, crown of thorns)
- Robes (robes of righteousness, garment of praise, white robes in heaven)
- Clothed with strength and dignity
- Clothe yourselves with compassion
- Armor of God

Light of the World

I love the metaphor of Matthew 5:14 ("You are the light of the world"), and I thought it would be fun to combine the two pieces of the sentence (light and world) into one picture. Because the verse is bold and direct, I decided to use acrylic paints instead of watercolors to achieve a strong, smooth look instead of a soft, flowy one.

For this project, you'll need:

- Flat brush
- Round brush for fine details
- Black acrylic paint
- White acrylic paint
- Blue acrylic paint

1. To begin, dip your flat brush into black acrylic paint (I'm using Master's Touch Permanent Black). Starting at the top left corner, paint all the way down the margin, working right up to the words and edge of the page.

2. After your black paint has completely dried, take your round paintbrush and dip it into white acrylic paint (I'm using Master's Touch Titanium White). I used the same Pentel water brush I use for watercolor, because I'm very familiar with the way it paints. Because this lightbulb drawing has some small lines inside, I wanted to use a brush I can easily control.

3. To draw the lightbulb, go about 2.5 inches down your margin and paint the beginnings of a circle, with a wide opening at the bottom. Then lengthen out the bottom about another half inch, closing it with a curved line. To draw the metal socket, paint four to five more curved lines underneath, connecting them on the sides. These lines will be close together and get gradually shorter in length toward the bottom of the socket. The wire filament inside the bulb is made up of two thin lines, crisscrossing over each other twice, with vertical lines connecting it to the metal socket at the bottom.

4. Finally, draw a map of the world on the lightbulb, as if it were a globe. Don't worry about this being geographically perfect; a general look of a map will do just fine!

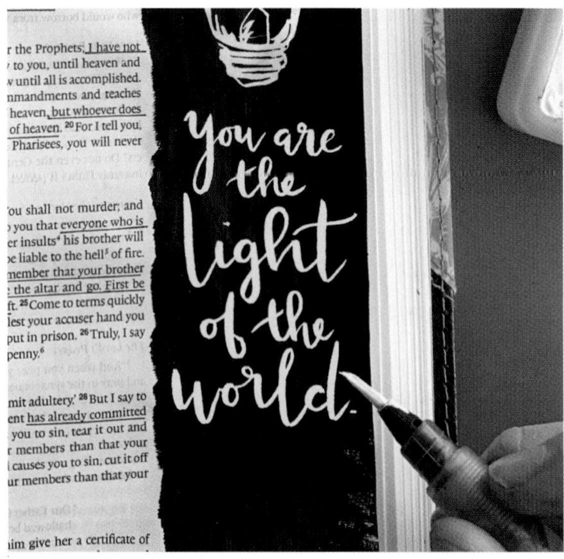

5. While your bulb is drying, paint the verse underneath. I stuck with my white paint and the same Pentel water brush, but you could change colors if you prefer variation. I chose to write the words "light" and "world" slightly larger on their own line because these were the words I wanted to emphasize.

6. After your bulb and words are completely dry, color the continents of your globe with a different acrylic paint. I chose Master's Touch Lake Blue, and I continued to use my water brush because of its small size and familiarity.

More Precious than Jewels

Proverbs 3:15 has filled me with wonder since I was a little girl. I remember playing dress-up and wanting to cover myself head to toe with every piece of plastic jewelry we had—crystal necklaces, emerald rings, pearl bracelets, and the golden, ruby crown that always gave me a headache. Yet the Bible says that there is something more precious than jewels: wisdom. Whenever life tempts me to feel envious of something like popularity, wealth, or talent, I bring this verse to the forefront of my mind, asking God to replace that envy with a greater request: a desire for more wisdom. According to this verse below, none of those other things can compare to wisdom.

I love illustrating jewels because of their brilliant colors and geometric shapes, and because (like flowers) no two jewels are the same. Each one varies in cut, size, color, and shape. Jewels are also one exception to the "source of light" rule I cover in Chapter 4. Since they reflect light from within and from each other, jewels and crystals shine radiantly in all directions. They can feel a bit complicated at first, but let yourself feel free from any pressure to "get them right." Whatever geometric shape you draw is exactly right, because it's totally possible for a jewel to look like what you create.

For this project, you'll need:

- Pencil
- Eraser
- A variety of jewel-toned colored pencils
- White colored pencil for blending
- White gel pen

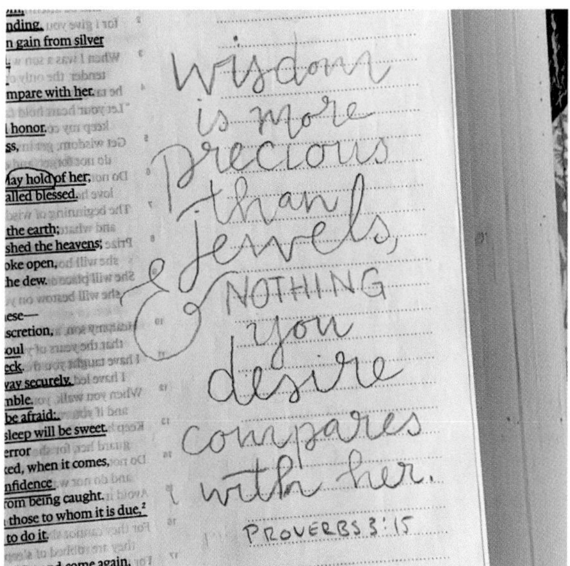

1. Use your pencil to write out the verse, centering it on the page. I chose to do simple cursive lettering, using an ampersand symbol for the word "and" to make it a bit more interesting, and capitalizing the word "nothing" for emphasis.

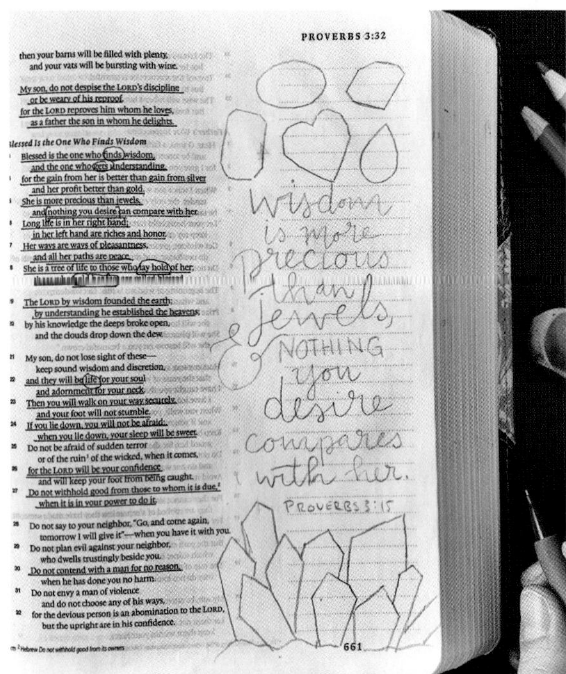

2. Draw the outlines for several types of jewels. The five jewels at the top of the page are simple shapes, including an oval, rectangle, heart, diamond, and teardrop. While I originally planned to make these shapes more geometric (you can see that I drew the heart with jagged lines), my final product has smooth lines for all of the outlines.

3. To make the crystals at the bottom of the page, begin by drawing a rocky baseline where all of your crystals will "sit." Next, draw several triangle shapes that point in various directions. These triangles should be different heights and shouldn't close on the bottom. Then, beginning with the shortest triangles, draw lines connecting the bottom two points of the triangle to the baseline. Each of these lines should angle slightly toward the center of the triangle, so that the crystals are wider at the top and narrower at the bottom.

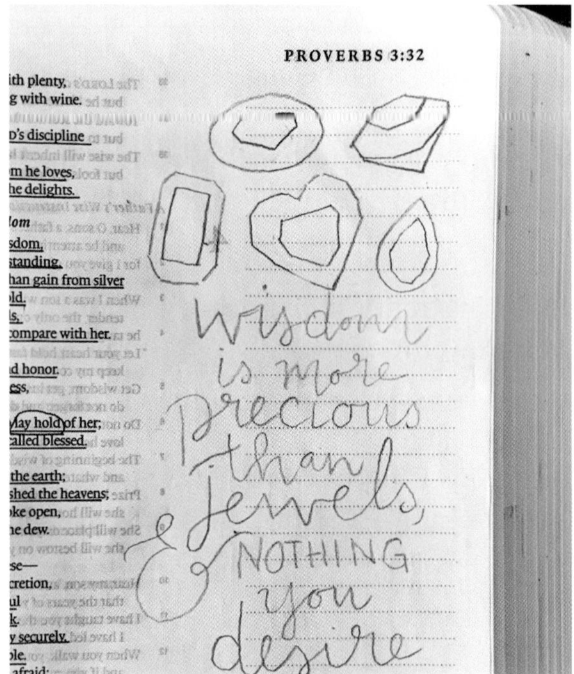

4. Next, begin to form the inside of the jewels. To define the top of the diamond, draw two lines that connect the left and the right side. Each of these lines will actually be made of three smaller slightly angled segments, which will help us divide the diamond into three sections in the next step. For the other four gems at the top, draw a basic geometric shape inside that mimics the outline (don't think too hard about this—the exact shape doesn't matter, as long as the shapes are angular instead of curvy).

5. There are three ways I like to draw the surfaces of the bottom crystals, and you can mix and match as much as you want. The first way is to draw an upside-down triangle that connects to the base of the top triangle. The second is to connect the right and left points of your initial triangle with a line that bends at an angle in two or three places. The third way is to copy the original crystal shape by drawing a smaller one inside your initial outline.

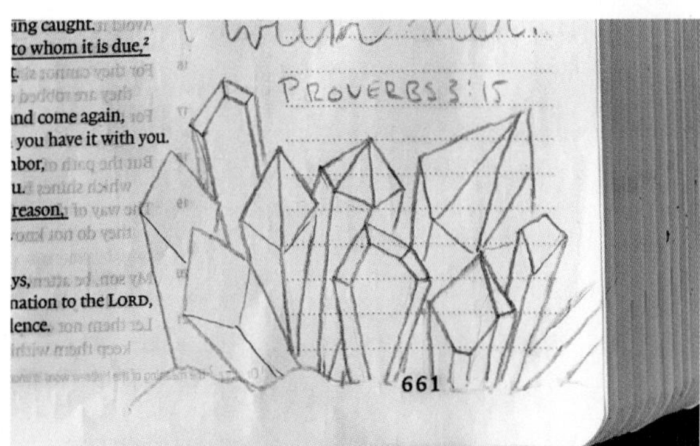

6. To finalize your gem shapes, connect every point on a line to another point. You can make this as busy or simple as you'd like! On the top jewels, I left the center of each shape empty but drew lots of connections between the surrounding points to form fairly busy gems. (Heads up: this made it a bit difficult to precisely color in later.) On the bottom crystals, I mainly focused on drawing long lines to connect each point to the floor. This lengthened my crystals without making them too complicated.

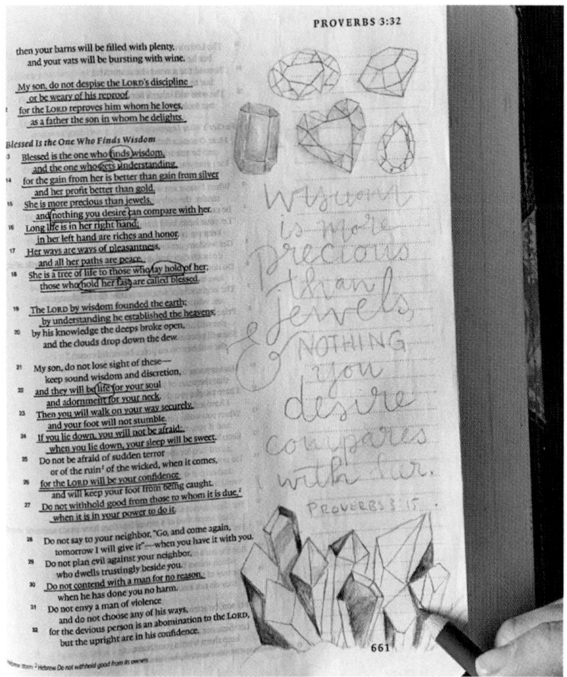

7. Here's where the fun part begins! Usually I recommend choosing just a few colors for an entire illustration in order to not make it too complicated, but with jewels, the more the merrier! On each section of my jewels, I used multiple colors in order to add dimension and light. Generally, I used darker shading at the points of the sections and lighter shading in the middle of each section. On flat surfaces, I colored diagonal gradients (where one color fades into another) to look like the large area is reflecting other crystals. You can see that I had finished coloring the heart gem and wasn't happy with it, so I erased my work. Colored pencils will only partially erase, but if you use the same color scheme on top of your erased portion, you'll never be able to tell the difference.

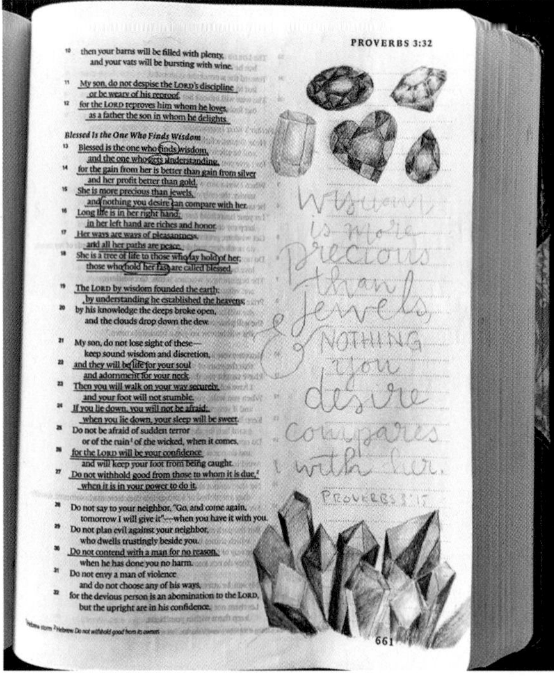

8. Continue coloring each section a different shade than the section next to it, varying between saturated, dark sections, and light, reflective sections.

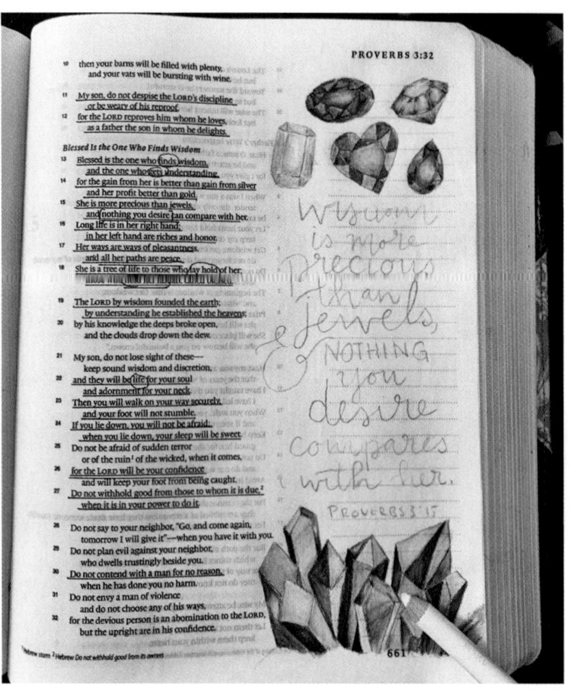

9. At this point, your shapes might look more like a patchwork quilt than shiny jewels. Don't worry! These next two steps help to transform them. First, take your white colored pencil and lightly go over all your work. With watercolor, I never use white because it makes my colors turn muddy and bland. But with colored pencils, white is a perfect way to blend multiple shades. This will help your jewels to begin having that smooth, glossy look.

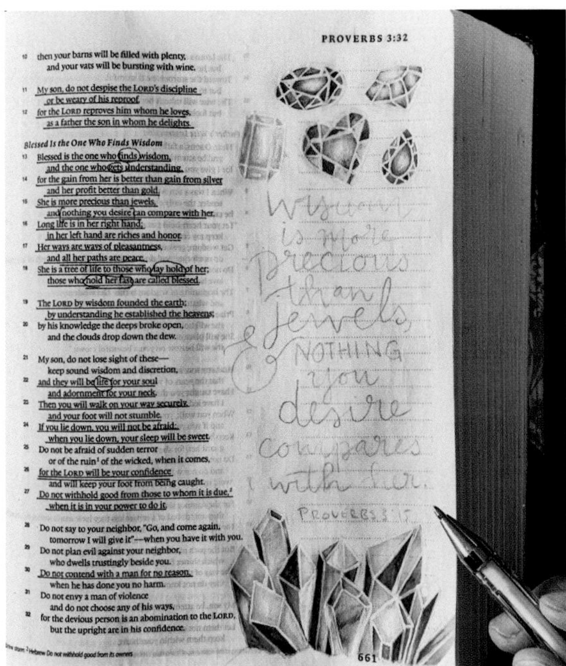

10. After finishing with your white colored pencil, you're ready for the secret weapon of jewel illustrations—a white gel pen! If you haven't used your gel pen in a while, it might seem like the ink won't stick on top of your colored pencils. Usually, you just need to let more ink build up in the tip (unless your pen is old and needs to be replaced). Once the ink is easily flowing, trace over all of your original lines. Be careful—gel pens are similar to paint and will smear if you touch them before they're dry. In some cases, this can be used to our advantage. For example, I also colored in the centers of my top jewels with the gel pen and then lightly patted them with my finger to slightly blend the white. In general, be generous with the gel pen! The more white you add, the more reflective your jewels will look.

11. To finish your page, trace over your verse with whatever colored pencil you like. Originally, I planned on doing an ombré effect from blue to pink by making each line of the verse a different shade. But halfway through, I accidentally picked up the wrong color and decided to go over all my lines with dark blue instead. Because I felt like I still needed a hint of pink at the bottom of the page, I lightly shaded the negative space surrounding the crystals with the same pink colored pencil that I used on the top heart.

Chapter Twelve

BIBLE STUDY

you shall love the Lord your God with all of your...
MIND
Matthew 22:37

When I was in middle school, my dad inherited a family heirloom: an antique desk that once belonged to his grandfather. With concentrated excitement, he brought it into our house, gathered all four of us kids around, and told us a story. He had a vivid memory from his childhood, where he sat on his grandfather's lap and was shown a secret compartment inside this very desk, the hiding place for all of his grandfather's valuable objects and money. My dad remembered exactly where the secret compartment was, and when he knocked on that specific wood panel, it sounded airy instead of solid like the rest of the wood, further evidence that something might be inside. The only problem? My dad couldn't remember how to open it.

I cannot tell you how many hours I spent alongside my brother and sisters trying to get inside that secret compartment. We twisted every knob, pressed every board, pulled out every drawer, and ran our fingers along every groove. And then we reversed the order of all our actions in the event that touching everything in a certain sequence unlocked the panel. Unfortunately, we never decoded the desk, and because my dad is more sentimental than greedy, we've never taken a chainsaw to it. But my assumption is that if you came over to my parent's house for Christmas dinner, you'd likely want to take a crack at solving the mystery too. Hidden treasure is tantalizing for all of us, and people who try to find it become easily obsessed. They let it take up the entire energy of their minds, use every creative measure they know to obtain it, and understand their lives would be forever changed if they found it.

The Treasure of Scripture

The Bible tells us that God's kingdom is like a treasure. It compares His words to gold, silver, and jewels and tells us that everything else in our life should be considered loss in comparison to "the surpassing value of knowing Christ" (Philippians 3:8). Take a look at the following verses through the lens of a treasure hunt:

My son, if you receive my words and treasure up my commandments with you, making your ear attentive to wisdom and inclining your heart to understanding; yes, if you call out for insight and raise your voice for understanding, if you seek it like silver and search for it as for hidden treasures, then you will understand the fear of the LORD and find the knowledge of God.

(Proverbs 2:1–5)

The kingdom of heaven is like a treasure hidden in the field, which a man found and hid again; and from joy over it he goes and sells all that he has and buys that field. Again, the kingdom of heaven is like a merchant in search of fine pearls, who, on finding one pearl of great value, went and sold all that he had and bought it.

(Matthew 13:44–46)

. . . attaining to all the wealth that comes from the full assurance of understanding, resulting in a true knowledge of God's mystery, that is, Christ Himself, in whom are hidden all the treasures of wisdom and knowledge.

(Colossians 2:2–3)

When we realize the wealth of the words sitting in our laps, it changes the way we read the Bible. There isn't room for a lazy mind. There isn't the option to pick it up here and there, flipping to random pages expecting to understand the treasure map. Instead, there's an urgency to know the words. There's a plan to figure out the information. There's late-night learning, turning phrases over and over in our minds, consulting with others, and then acting on what we discover. There's Bible study.

Using Our Journaling Bibles for Study

Bible study is my favorite way to use my journaling Bible. Memorizing verses and illustrating passages is a deeply soul-nourishing way to engage with the Word of God, but there is nothing I prefer more than using the wide margins of my Bible to dig deeply into the text.

Because the Bible is a book that I'm basing my entire life around—the lens through which I process my past, engage my present, and plan my future—I want to *really* know what it says. I want to spend significant energy mining the verses, separating the words out so I see the sentences clearly, connecting the dots of each individual story in order to see the final grand picture. One way I do this is through valuing context.

In her book *Women of the Word*, Jen Wilkin highlights a way that many of us grow up reading our Bibles, calling it the "pinball approach." Although we have a genuine desire to know God, we habitually read the Bible by opening up to random pages, reading a verse here and there and then flipping to a new spot. She says,

> *When we read this way, we treat the Bible with less respect than we would give to a simple textbook. Imagine trying to master algebra by randomly reading for ten minutes each day from whatever paragraph in the textbook your eyes happened to fall on . . . you'd lose momentum fast (and be very bad at algebra). A well-rounded approach to Bible study takes into account how any given passage fits into the bigger picture of what the Bible has to say.*

In college, I decided to read the Bible from cover to cover for the first time. While I don't think the Bible always needs to be read this way, I couldn't believe how many stories I had never connected until I purposefully linked each of the stories to the ones before and after them. For example, I never knew that Ruth was King David's great-grandmother, or understood the devastation of the destruction of the temple. By reading the books within their own context (understanding what the author meant to say to the original readers, in their specific moment in history) and by reading them in the context of the whole Bible, I grew a love and appreciation for the treasure of Scripture that I had never experienced before.

So how can we apply this to our journaling Bibles? Here are six Bible-study strategies that have helped me discover the riches of Scripture through simple investigation exercises:

Who, What, When, Where, Why, and How

On the title page of each book of the Bible, draw an easy chart to help you value the context of what you're reading and develop a clear picture of the purposes of the book. Use your ruler and pen to draw two columns (one thin and one thick) with six rows. In the first column, use your pen or alphabet stamps to write six words: Who, What, When, Where, Why, and How. Because these words vary in length, I stamped them on their sides so that the column could be thin and uniform, helping the page look clean and giving myself more space to write the answers. When you're studying the book, you'll use the second column to respond to each of the following questions:

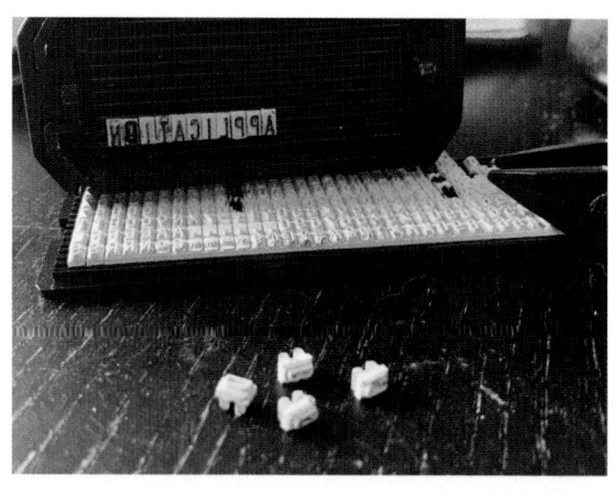

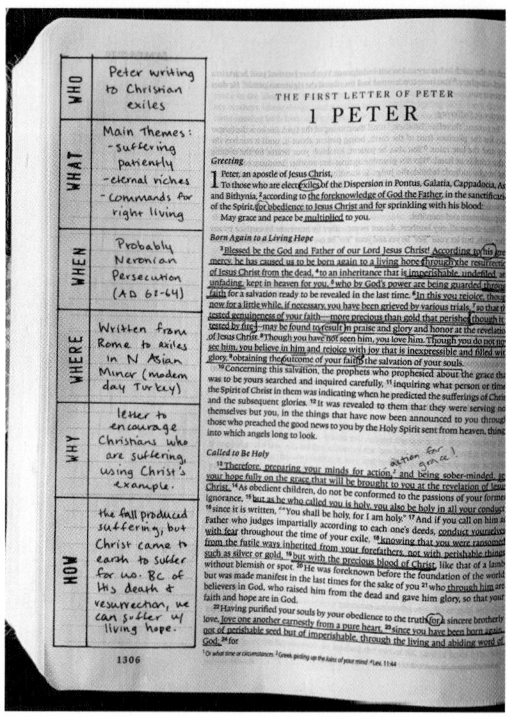

WHO: Who is the author? Whom are they writing to?

WHAT: What are the main themes of the book? Are there any keywords?

WHEN: When was the book written?

WHERE: Where is the author writing from? Where is he writing to?

WHY: Why did the author write this book?

HOW: How does this book contribute to the master story of the Bible?

Sometimes these answers are easily found just by reading the book. For example, it's clear that the book of James is written by James. But sometimes, we need to do a little bit of outside research in order to find the answers we're looking for. I usually consult my ESV study Bible first, and then if I still can't find the answers, I'll look online. It's always good to cross-reference a couple of different websites (such as www.Bible.org and www.enduringword.com) to make sure we're getting the right information.

An example of this from my own Bible is the book of 1 Peter. This has been one of my favorite books of the Bible for a long time, and I've underlined almost every passage. Yet the day that I decided to apply the "Who, What, When, Where, Why, and How" strategy, I discovered something significant within the very first question that changed the way I saw the entire book. Peter wrote his letter to Christians living in spiritual exile (people who were totally rejected by their communities for their faith in Christ). Even though the word "exiles" is bluntly stated in the first verse, I had always glossed over the introductory greeting, eager to get to the rest of the book.

Yet by doing so, I had missed a treasure in front of me. Read these famous passages from 1 Peter in light of knowing that they were written to outcasts:

> *In this you rejoice, though now for a little while, if necessary, you have been grieved by various trials, so that the tested genuineness of your faith—more precious than gold that perishes though it is tested by fire—may be found to result in praise and glory and honor at the revelation of Jesus Christ.*
>
> (1 Peter 1:6–7)

> *But you are a chosen race, a royal priesthood, a holy nation, a people for his own possession, that you may proclaim the excellencies of Him who called you out of darkness into his marvelous light.*
>
> (1 Peter 2:9)

> *Finally, all of you, have unity of mind, sympathy, brotherly love, a tender heart, and a humble mind. Do not repay evil for evil or reviling for reviling, but on the contrary, bless, for to this you were called . . ."*
>
> (1 Peter 3:8–9)

By doing the investigative work of understanding the original purpose for the letter, I now see the gems of 1 Peter in a different light. I recognize that the people who received this letter were suffering life-altering rejection, and so I marvel when Peter affirms their royal identity, and I feel challenged when Peter exhorts them to repay evil with a blessing.

Word Mapping

Another way I mine the Word of God for treasure is by paying attention to keywords, or words that are repeated within a short section of text. Repetition indicates that the author is trying to emphasize something specific, and so it's worth it for me to take time to explore. Famous examples are the word "love" in 1 Corinthians 13, "faith" in Hebrews 11, and "word" in Psalm 119. In the sample below, my little sister pointed out to me how many times the phrase "In Christ" is used in Ephesians 1. By doing a word map of each phrase, I clearly see the eternal riches we have as believers in Jesus.

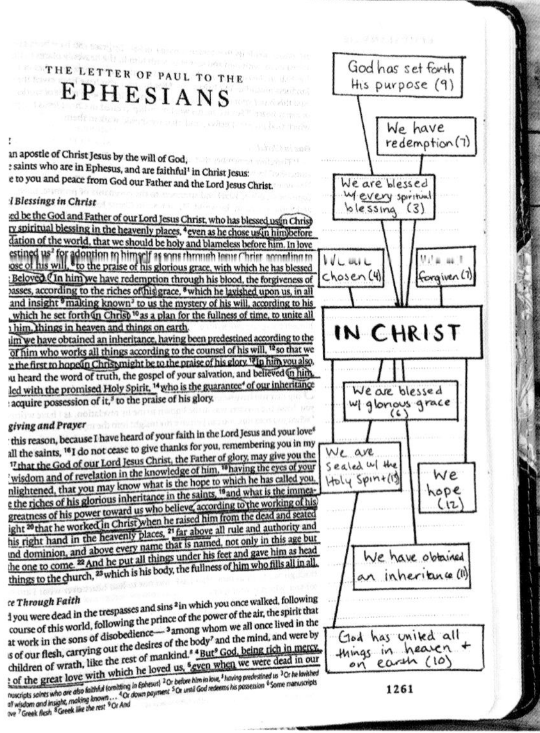

To make a word map in your Bible, first identify which keyword you want to study. Next, use your ruler to create a large rectangle in the center of your margin, and then draw the keyword inside the rectangle with your brush pen. On a separate sheet of paper, write down each of the times that the keyword is used in the passage. Then, using a pencil so you can easily erase and move words around, begin to stagger the phrases around the center rectangle. (Sometimes it's helpful to first do this on a separate sheet of paper to ensure that you can fit everything cleanly in a small space. If there are too many phrases, I also recommend putting your word map on a piece of cardstock and using washi tape to secure it to the correct page.) Once you're happy with the way everything is placed, trace over your words with a Micron 01 pen, draw rectangles around each phrase, and use your ruler to draw a straight line from the center keyword to all of the individual phrases.

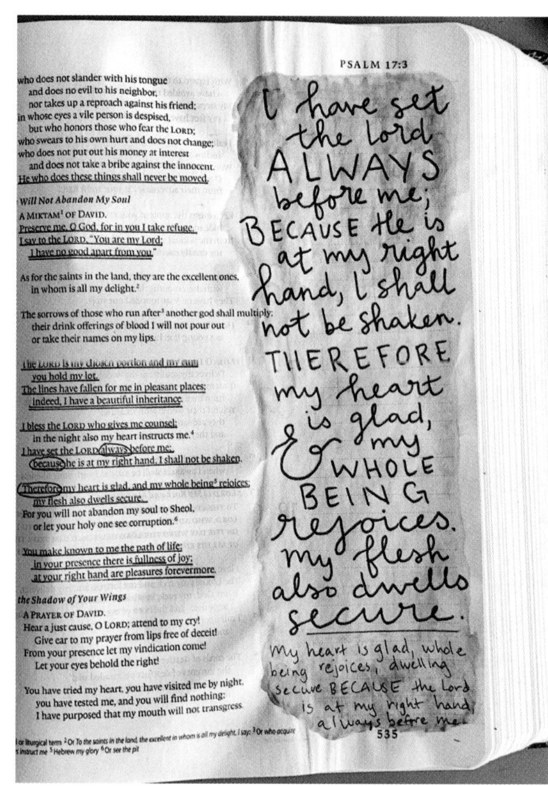

Transition Words

A third way I study the Bible is by focusing on transition words, such as "therefore," "and," "now," "since," "so that," "for," "but," "so," "then," and "because." These words signal that there is a connection between two thoughts, and if I'm not paying attention, I might gloss over that connection. For example, in Psalm

16:8–9, the word "therefore" connects two verses that are frequently memorized independently of each other:

When I pay attention to this transition word, I can understand the true treasure of the verse: My heart is glad, my whole being rejoices, and I dwell secure *because* I have set the Lord always before me.

One way to etch keywords into your mind is to ask a fun question:

What is the THEREFORE there for?

Because I've memorized this question, it stops me in my tracks every time I come across the word "therefore." Then, I go back and explore the transition. And even though it's not nearly as fun, this question can apply to all of the transition words.

To emphasize transition words in your Bible, first underline or highlight the transition word in your text. Then, in the margin, write the verse, leaving enough space at the bottom for a verse explanation. After asking yourself how the transition word helps two thoughts connect, write down your response.

Timelines

Sometimes it can take us several weeks to read through one book of the Bible, especially as we're making our way through the Old Testament. Reading through all of the different genealogies, prophecies, traditions, and prayers can make our brain feel a bit jumbled, and it's easy to lose track of the main story. A truly helpful way for me to organize the information in my mind is to draw out a timeline. This helps me latch onto the main events of the book in their correct order, bringing clarity and simplicity to the big-picture view of the book.

A timeline won't make sense in every book of the Bible because books like Psalms, Proverbs, and many letters of the New Testament don't have a defined sequence of events. My favorite books for timelines include Genesis through Job, Daniel, and Jonah in the Old Testament and Matthew through Acts in the New Testament.

To make a timeline, find an unused margin in the book you're studying and turn your Bible sideways. In the example from Genesis above, I used two pages for my timeline because there are so many major events in the book. First, draw out a header at the top (i.e., along the side of the page) with your pen or colored pencils. Next, use your ruler to draw a long, straight line, positioning it so that there is enough space on both the top and the bottom to write down events. I suggest using a Micron 05 pen for the actual timeline and dots and a Micron 01 pen for your writing.

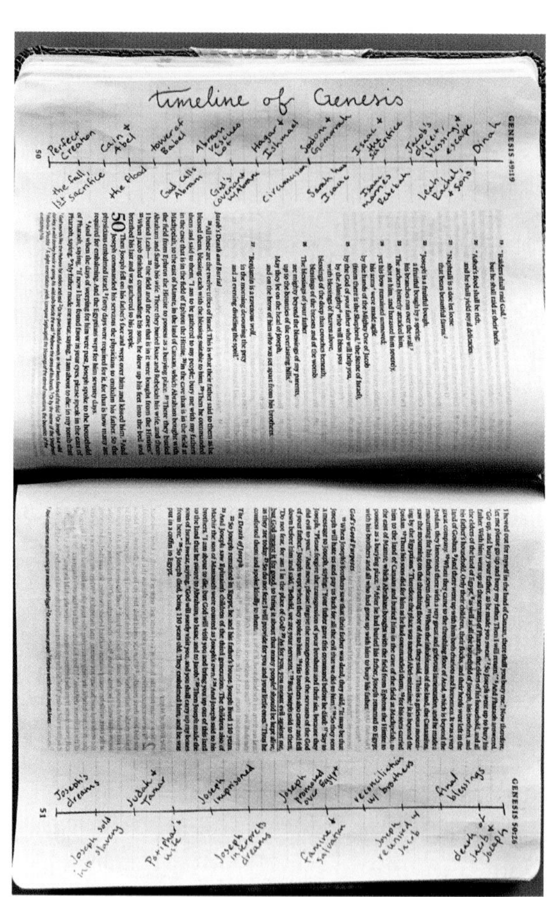

I recommend filling out your timeline in one of two ways. The first option is to read through the entire book, and then after you finish, use the timeline as a way to conduct a massive book review. Skim back through the chapters, and each time you come to a key event, jot it down on your timeline. This option is great for picking up the small details through your initial read, and then cementing the main events in your mind when you go back through the book.

The second option is to write key events on your timeline as you come across them. As you're reading, pay attention to any significant developments in the story, such as births, deaths, marriages, wars, betrayals, miracles, and covenants. As you find them, simply flip to your timeline and write them down.

Color Coding

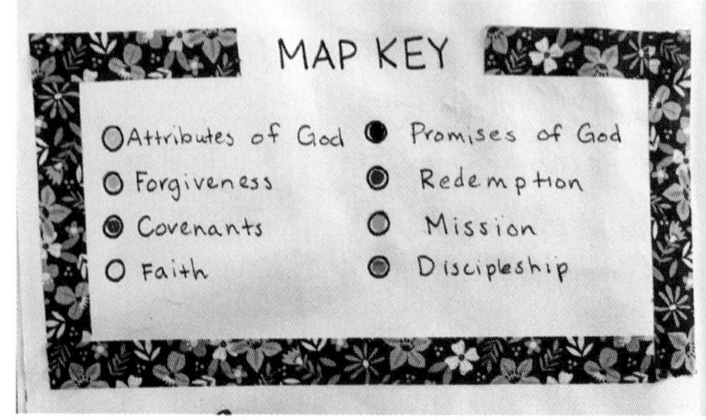

The Bible is filled with specific themes that surface over and over, continually redirecting us to understand the master story of Scripture. In order to trace these themes from book to book, it can help to color code them as we find them. This serves two purposes. One, when we're actively searching for the major themes of the Bible, we're more likely to find them! You can continue to think of this as treasure hunting. Through this activity, we're color coding the jewels we find. A second reason for this exercise is that you might want to do an in-depth study of a specific topic at some point. When you already have it color coded, it's significantly easier to flip through your Bible and pull out the passages you need.

Examples of themes to color code include:

- The attributes of God (traits such as all-knowing, all-powerful, and eternal)
- The promises of God
- The fall
- Redemption
- Restoration
- Forgiveness
- Covenants (binding promises made between God and His people)
- Faith
- Heaven
- Prophecy

To color code your Bible, you'll need an easy reminder of the connection between your colors and themes, and keeping in line with our treasure analogy, this is actually called a Map Key! In the front of your Bible, designate a small space to write down the themes you want to track, along with that theme's assigned color; this will let you see at a quick glance what each color means. Over the course of your Bible-reading journey, you'll most likely misplace or use up the pens, highlighters, or colored pencils that you initially used to color code your themes. For this reason, I recommend choosing common colors that can be easily matched with a different pen, pencil, or highlighter. I also used washi tape as my Map Key border because I know I might add more themes and colors to it in the future. Washi tape can easily be peeled off and replaced to make room for new themes.

When marking up your Bible with colors, you can use different types of coloring tools depending on how you want your page to look. Highlighters generally color over the entire text, pens underline the sentences, and colored pencils can do both. I enjoy using different-colored pens, and I usually have a bookmark in my Bible that I use as a ruler to keep my underlining straight and clean.

Application Questions

So far, we've discussed using the opening page of each book to ask context questions and using the body margins of the book for keywords, transition words, timelines, and color coding. Now we'll discuss using the final page of each book to ask application questions.

Before learning about strategic ways to study the Bible, I generally approached 100 percent of my Bible-reading time with personal application in mind. With a heart that genuinely wanted to grow, I read chapter after chapter through the lens of questions such as "How does this verse apply to my situation?" and "What does this teach me about myself?" But in her book *Women of the Word*, Jen Wilkin presents an important and obvious truth: The Bible is not about me. It is about God. We do not need to write ourselves into every page in order to feel captivated by the story. Doing so can leave us confused and frustrated with what we see in Scripture, and, ultimately, it can cause us to miss out on fixing our eyes on the actual hero of the Bible: God.

Applying Scripture is a vital and exhilarating piece of growing in our love for the Lord, and making a personal connection to the whole of the Bible is crucial for allowing it to transform us. But application should always be done through placing Christ at center stage and purposefully moving ourselves to the background. Doing so helps us reinforce all the Bible-study strategies we've already mentioned: it opens our eyes to the true context and meaning of the verse, because we're not trying to nicely fit everything we read into our current cultural understanding. It helps us do the hard work of analyzing keywords, transition words, timelines, and themes, because we're not rushing to make everything about ourselves before we fully understand what the verses are saying. And finally, it helps us to grow confidence in the Lord, because when we place Him rightfully in the center of our minds, we finally understand our identity as Christians in light of who He is: our Savior, our Redeemer, our Friend, our Father. Elevating God to the forefront of our Bible reading doesn't diminish our connection to Scripture, halt our personal growth, or make us detached readers; instead, it helps us to truly discover our own infinite value as His children.

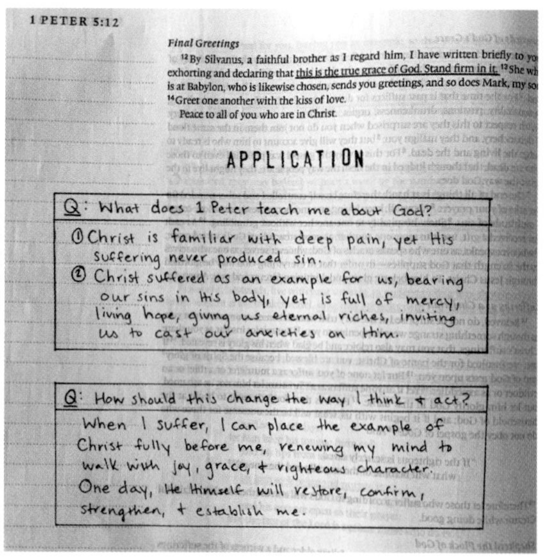

Here are two of the application questions I always ask at the end of each book:

1. What did this teach me about God?
2. How should this change the way I think and act?

The first question helps direct my understanding back toward God, remembering to constantly place Him as the main character in every chapter. By focusing on His personality (traits like His kindness, patience, compassion, and righteousness), His actions (miracles, discipline, judgment, and forgiveness), and His intentions for His people (reconciliation, friendship, and a new earth), I can better answer the second question. I can see myself clearly in light of who God is, and I can ask Him to transform me into His image. Then, I can work to implement changes in my life, trusting that God will carry out the good work that He is doing in me.

"Books I've Read" Coloring Sheet

For this final project, I wanted to create a fun, interactive page on the inside of our Bible covers that we can use as encouragement to keep making our way through Scripture. Sometimes when we sit down with our Bibles, there can be a feeling of total overwhelm at the size of the book, and it feels like it's impossible to get through it, let alone internalize it and understand its truths. By seeing the individual books and coloring them in as we go, we can feel a godly sense of achievement over what we've read and motivation to continue digging in.

For this project, you'll need:

- Ruler
- Pencil
- Eraser
- Micron 03 and 01 pens
- Watercolor paint (I'm using a teal shade)
- Colored pencils to color in the books you've read

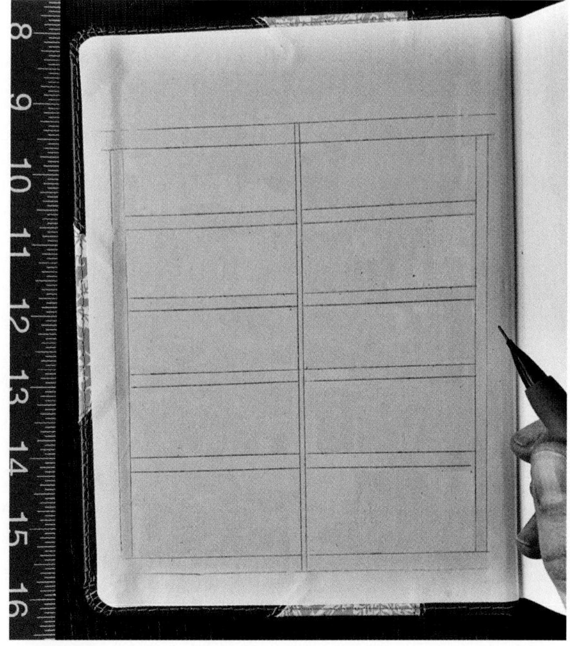

1. To begin, open up your Bible to the inside of the cover, and use your ruler and pencil to create the outline of a bookcase. Leaving about an inch at the top for a future page header, draw two horizontal, parallel lines across your page, about a quarter inch apart (the precise measurement isn't that important; there just needs to be enough space for you to write something between the lines). Then, draw three pairs of vertical parallel lines—on the left, center, and right—dividing the bookcase in two. These left and right divisions will organize your books into the Old Testament and New Testament. Connect all of these together with another pair of horizontal lines at the bottom, forming the base of your bookcase.

2. Next, draw the shelves. Inside the bookcase, draw four pairs of horizontal parallel lines, breaking in the middle for the center beam. Each shelf should be thick enough for you to write a label on. The shelves will represent the various categories into which we'll organize the books of the Bible.

3. The next step is to draw the books. Before I began, I did some research on how the books of the Bible are organized, and then I based the design of my bookcase on the number of books in each category:

Old Testament

- Law: 5 books
- History: 12 books
- Wisdom: 5 books
- Minor prophets: 5 books
- Major prophets: 12 books

New Testament

- Gospels: 4 books
- History: 1 book
- Paul's letters to churches: 9 books
- Paul's letters to individuals: 4 books
- General letters: 8 books
- Apocalyptic: 1 book

Each shelf gets one category, except for the top right shelf on the New Testament side, where I put both the gospels and history.

To create the books, simply take your ruler and form small rectangle boxes on each shelf. Make sure that each book is thick enough to write a title on. I decided to vary the thickness, height, and orientation of my books because it made the shelves more visually appealing, but if you prefer a clean look, you can draw them straight across. I also left spaces to add cute decorations on the shelves that had fewer books.

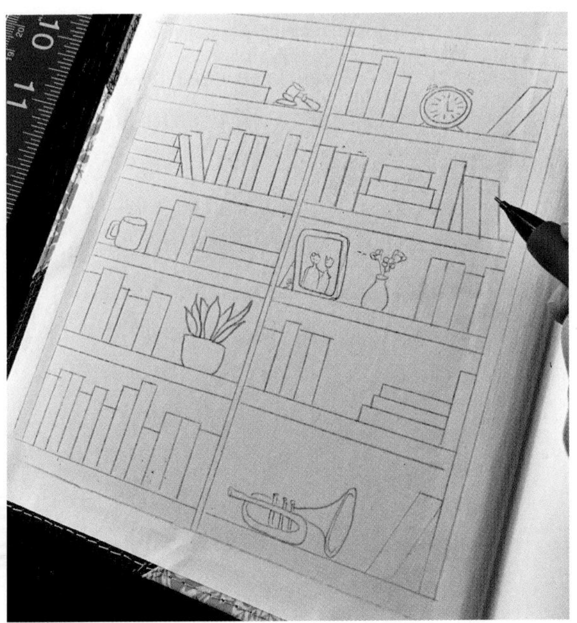

4. Next, add some cute decorations to the empty spaces on your shelf. Where it made sense, I drew items that had to do with the category of the shelf, like a judge's gavel for "Law," a picture of two friends for "Paul's Letters to Individuals," and I couldn't resist when my husband recommended that I draw a trumpet for "Apocalyptic." But these could be anything! If flowers and succulents are your jam, fill the whole thing up with them. Other ideas could include a jewelry stand, pen holder, painting, baskets, or whatever you have on your bookcases at home.

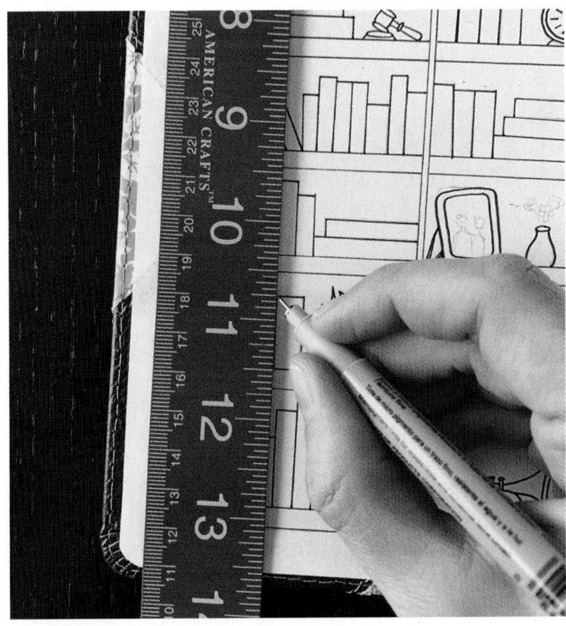

5. Using your ruler, trace back over all of your pencil lines with a pen. I recommend a Micron 03 pen because it will be thick enough to make bold lines, but thin enough that it won't take up too much of the negative space inside your books, leaving room for the book names.

6. Using a small or medium round brush and the watercolor of your choice, paint the back panels of your bookshelf. To begin, soak your brush in clean water, and then saturate it in the paint. I recommend starting at the top corners and getting slightly lighter as you head toward the center, which will add dimension to your picture.

7. After the watercolor has completely dried, it's time to fill in all the labels. I chose to only use two fonts, cursive and all caps, because the page is already busy and I didn't want additional fonts to make it confusing. I wrote all of these words with a ruler and pencil first, and then I traced them with a Micron 02 pen. At the top of your page, write "Books I've Read." At the top of the left column, write "Old Testament," and at the top right column, write "New Testament." Next, label each shelf with its book category.

8. Turn your Bible sideways and write the names of all the books. I decided to use name abbreviations for books over five letters long because I didn't want the writing to look squished.

9. Next, erase your pencil marks. Then use colored pencils to color in the books of the Bible you've already read.

Celebrate Finishing the Bible!

When you finish that final sentence in your Bible and color in that last little rectangle, it is time to CELEBRATE. I'm talking triple chocolate cake, balloons, confetti, and friends (if a parade is an option, make it happen!). We have events for all sorts of achievements in our lives and throw barbeques for holidays we don't even understand; you can feel totally thrilled to host a party for completing one of the hardest but most edifying tasks of your life. Finishing your entire Bible is a tremendous milestone, and it will potentially take you a couple of years, even with consistent reading. The edifying, supernatural journey you've taken to love the Lord with all your heart, soul, and mind is worth a suspended moment in time to celebrate. Congratulations!

APPENDIX

For more information on how to study the Bible:

BibleProject. www.bibleproject.com.

Broocks, Rice, Steve Murrell, and Ed Stetzer. *The Purple Book: Biblical Foundations for Building Strong Disciples*. Updated ed. Grand Rapids, MI: Zondervan, 2017.

Carafano, Vinnie. *Knowing God's Heart: Missions and Evangelism*. Seattle, WA: YWAM Publishing, 2013.

Lewis, Alan J. *Pathways Bible Study Method: A Better Way to Do Bible Study . . .* Self-published, Amazon.com Services, 2015.

Robert, Vaughan. *God's Big Picture: Tracing the Storyline of the Bible*. Downers Grove, IL: InterVarsity Press, 2002.

Wilkin, Jen. *Women of the Word: How to Study the Bible with Both Our Hearts and Our Minds*. Wheaton, IL: Crossway, 2019.

For more information on creative lettering:

Website of Stefan Kunz, www.stefankunz.com.

For more inspiration on combining art with Scripture:

Raynor, Jordan. *Called to Create: A Biblical Invitation to Create, Innovate, and Risk*. Grand Rapids, MI: Baker Books, 2017.

Simons, Ruth Chou. *Gracelaced: Discovering Timeless Truths through Seasons of the Heart*. Eugene, OR: Harvest House Publishers, 2017.

To find more of my artwork, you can follow me on Instagram @kristindurandesigns or visit my Etsy shop at www.etsy.com/shop/kristindurandesigns.

ACKNOWLEDGMENTS

Dan, I cannot thank you enough for how well you loved and supported me while I wrote this book. We knew it would be a challenge for me to take on this project with a toddler, but we didn't know it would also be in the middle of a quarantine and that I would be pregnant. Your incredible encouragement, love, patience, and care for Cassius and me these last few months has blown me away.

Cassius, you absolutely explode my heart with joy. I couldn't love you a single ounce more. And to the little one growing inside of me while I wrote this book: I can't wait to meet you. I already love you so much.

Mom, Dad, Jimmy, Kimmie, and Julie: I'm so incredibly grateful that I grew up in a home that honors imagination, encourages creativity, and loves the Bible. Thank you for brainstorming, listening, celebrating, proofreading, and acting as a soundboard for this book. Y'all came through strong. And Austin and Julie, thank you for taking a whole day to make me coffee and go line by line through my outline with ideas and recommendations.

Gabe and Martha Duran: I truly won the in-laws jackpot! Thank you so much for your constant encouragement and your overflowing love and support.

Tiffany, Tessa, Elissa, and Calah: Your friendships have meant the world to me for years, but our Marco Polo chats are what got me through the last few months. I'm so lucky to have y'all in my corner.

Carrie, I'm so grateful that you were a few steps ahead of me in this book-writing adventure. Thank you for your sound advice, direction, and friendship. Finley, thank you for playing with Cassius so I could get some work done. We love our Fin Fin.

Every Nation Ministries, The Springs Church, and Mosaic Church Austin: You have grown my love for Scripture and discipleship in ways I never dreamed. I pray this book is used to engage, establish, equip, and empower girls with the gospel.

Pastor Jack Hammans, you are a gift from God to our family. Thank you for reading through these pages with a theological fine-tooth comb.

Jimmy Feuille, thank you for looking over all of the legal things. I wouldn't have felt confident moving forward if it weren't for your help.

Claire Sielaff, your initial email inviting me to write this book was a dream come true. Thank you for choosing me! Tyanni Niles, thank you for walking me through the whole process and giving me encouragement and feedback. Anne Healey, thank you for your thoughtful and thorough edits, especially in the instructional sections. You helped bring wonderful clarity to my writing.

And God, I love Your word. I hope this book honors You and makes You smile. Thank You for creativity. Thank You for imagination. I love You, and I love the life You've given me.

ABOUT THE AUTHOR

KRISTIN DURAN is a self-taught artist living in Austin, Texas, with her high-school-sweetheart husband, son, two dogs, and a herd of cows that occasionally breaks into her backyard. She grew up in a missionary family, and by the time she was eighteen, they had done missionary work in fourteen different countries. Kristin is passionate about Scripture memory, and throughout her life she has used both journaling and art to dive deeply into the Word of God. You can find her in her little home studio, toddler scrunching up rough-draft paper at her feet, as she paints out verses and makes them available online. For Bible journaling inspiration, you can follow her on Instagram at @kristindurandesigns.

GENESIS 14:11
Abram and Melchizedek
God's Covenant with Abram
GENESIS 16:13
You-are-the-God-Who-Sees
Genesis 16:13